Photo: Daisy Steers

ANNA REYNOLDS

Anna's writing career includes journalism for the *Times,* the *Guardian,* and the *Observer;* award-winning short stories for anthologies, non-fiction and novels; and writing for stage, screen, radio, dance and opera. Her stage work has been seen nationally at venues including Riverside Hammersmith, Trestle Theatre, Theatre by the Lake and many other UK spaces; internationally including New York, Los Angeles, Athens, Berlin, Oslo, Paris and Reykjavik; and she has won Time Out, Writer's Guild and other awards.

Plays include *Jordan* (Lilian Baylis Theatre), *Wild Things* (Salisbury Playhouse), *Red* (Clean Break Theatre Company), *Deep Joy* (Mercury Theatre Colchester), *Skin Hunger* (Battersea Arts Centre), *SoulPlay* (The Place/ Watford Palace), *Precious* (West Yorkshire Playhouse), *Look At Me* (Theatre Centre), also published by Aurora Metro Press, and the opera *Push!* for Tete-a-Tete.

Anna is a Royal Literary Fund Fellow currently at University College London Hospitals Trust, an editor/mentor for Cornerstones Literary Consultancy, and fundraises for and produces her own arts community projects.

First published in the UK in 2023 by Aurora Metro Publications Ltd.

80 Hill Rise, Richmond, TW10 6UB

www.aurorametro.com   info@aurorametro.com

X:@aurorametro FB: /AuroraMetroBooks

Nothing on Earth © Anna Reynolds 2023

Production photography © Greta Zabulyte 2023

Music for 'Once They Are Aroused' © Helen Chadwick 2023. info@pursuedbyabear.co.uk for rights / further information queries.

Cover images by Steph Pyne Design; imagery includes Géhane Strehler (photo by Ian Phillips)

Cover design copyright Aurora Metro Books © 2023

Editing & Production: Cheryl Robson

All rights are strictly reserved.

For rights enquiries including performing rights, please contact the publisher: rights@aurorametro.com

No part of this publication may be reproduced, stored in or introduced into a retrieval system, or transmitted in any form, or by any means (electronic, mechanical, photocopying, recording or otherwise) without the prior permission of the publisher. Any person who does any unauthorised act in relation to this publication may be liable to criminal prosecution and civil claims for damages.

This paperback is sold subject to the condition that it shall not, by way of trade or otherwise, be lent, resold, hired out, or otherwise circulated without the publisher's prior consent in any form of binding or cover other than that in which it is published and without a similar condition being imposed on the subsequent purchaser.

Printed in the UK by 4edge Ltd, Essex on sustainably resourced paper.

ISBNs:

978-1-912430-99-4 (print)

978-1-911501-21-3 (ebook)

NOTHING ON EARTH

BY

ANNA REYNOLDS

AURORA METRO BOOKS

Nothing on Earth is dedicated to the memory of my friend Richard, who inspired the play and so much else with his compassion, curiosity, wisdom and strange attitude towards proverbs.

CONTENTS

WRITING THE PLAY	7
PLAYTEXT	9
ABOUT THE PRODUCTION	85
WORKSHOP RESOURCES	96
COMPANY INFORMATION	109

Writing the Play
Anna Reynolds

Nothing on Earth takes its title from the legendary speech by Emmeline Pankhurst given in 1913 in Connecticut, where she speaks of the options for women on the issue of the vote; freedom or death. 'When women are determined... nothing on earth and nothing in heaven will make them give way'.

A hundred years later, in association with Trestle, I was creating a Heritage Lottery Fund project called Hertfordshire's Hidden Heroines. This aimed to discover, re-discover, elevate and celebrate some of the 'lost' or hidden women of the county of Hertfordshire, and three extraordinary heroines stood out to me. The suffragette Constance Lytton who wondered what she should pack for prison, the explorer Violet Cressy-Marcks who calmly drank coffee while waiting to see if she would die of a snake bite, and the Edwardian balloonist Dolly Shepherd who made parachute descents in her bloomers. The detail was what appealed to me, but also the sheer scale of their courage, often going against the tide. Once the project ended, these women refused to leave my head, and set up camp in there, waiting...

Until 2016, when theatre director Rosamunde Hutt from Pursued By A Bear got in touch to ask me; would I like to write a play about women? I – and the women in my head – all leapt at the chance. And so *Nothing on Earth* was born.

At the beginning of 2019, I was a carer for my friend until he died, and the Covid pandemic obviously put a hold on the play's production. But in that hiatus, I realised that the heart of the play, the core character and theme, was related to my own experience of caring, and of loss, and of the courage that countless people began to find in themselves, and to draw from past stories of joy, high-flying, fear, love, failure and ultimately, going for it, whatever 'it' was...

Nothing on Earth has been the greatest joy to write, to be involved in, and to learn from, and I am grateful for the opportunity. I hope that someone else may take from it something of the sheer, staggering depths and heights that women dive to, swoop to and experience, in the past, present and future.

NOTHING ON EARTH

ANNA REYNOLDS

Characters

JADE a care home worker
DOLLY an Edwardian aerialist
CONSTANCE a suffragette
VIOLET an explorer
JUNE a care home resident
GRANDA JADE's grandad
MONSIEUR DOLLY's boss
AUNTY a marabou feather emporium owner
DOCTOR a medic
MAY a plane-builder
LORD VICTOR CONSTANCE's brother
WARDER in prison
BOUSHRA a pilot
MR VIOLET VIOLET's husband
CHILD VIOLET's child
SERVANT VIOLET's cook

This play can be performed by 5 actors, with actors doubling roles, or by as many actors as are available.

Certain main characters in the play are inspired by real people:

Violet Olivia Cressy-Marcks, nee Rutley, later Fisher (1895-1970) an explorer and pioneer originally living in Bushey.

Elizabeth 'Dolly' Shepherd (1886-1983) a young balloonist and aerial artist who hailed from Potters Bar.

Constance Lytton (1869-1923) an activist, writer and suffragette who lived in Knebworth House.

Victor Bulwer-Lytton, 2nd Earl of Lytton (1876-1947), brother of Constance

The poem *High Flight* by John Gillespie Magee Jr (1941) is used in the play.

DOLLY, JADE and *GRANDA* sing 'There is a Happy Land' by Andrew Young (1838).

Setting: The play is set in a care home. Past and present collides throughout.

ACT ONE

DOLLY, CONSTANCE and VIOLET are a Greek chorus of women preparing for a series of adventures which we will discover later... they are frantically or energetically or excitedly packing and organising and mobilising...

DOLLY Always remember to check everything thoroughly. Then check again. Every rope, every line, every time. ALWAYS... your life depends upon it

CONSTANCE They say you need plenty of books... a pen of course... Or is that a dangerous object... it should be, in the right hands

VIOLET Just stuff everything in the bloody bag and get out of here! The mule is leaving NOW!

DOLLY They say don't look down

VIOLET They say what's wrong with staying at home with your husband and children? I say, every bloody thing!

CONSTANCE They say women will not use the vote wisely

DOLLY They say don't look down but

CONSTANCE Look at all that... *life* out there that everyone else is living...

DOLLY ... You need to know where you're going or how will you get there?

VIOLET Just take what you need and the rest doesn't matter once you've set off! It's time!

DOLLY It's time!

CONSTANCE It's time...

They turn to stone revealing:

JADE sits outside; somewhere not very pleasant with fake plants, badly disguised industrial sized bins and a cigarette shelter. Nevertheless she is beautifully made up and presented, a rose among thorns...

A small plane can be heard, overhead, JADE looks up, follows it with her gaze.

JADE I miss you
I'll always miss you

Wherever I am, no matter how old I get, no matter
what happens to me from now on
Because...
You have been my everything
Always and in all ways
But that was then
And this...this has to be new
This is now.

She gets up, puts on her care home uniform; lanyard, tabard, badge. Looks at us in a very honest, direct way. Buzzers start to sound, alarms, medical bleepers, the sound of running feet, trolleys, wheelchairs, lifts clanking... other noises of care home life...

JADE   I love my job.
My *new* job.
It's probably the best job I've ever had.
Although the old one was pretty good... But-
Times change. Things happen. And I've got what they call *transferable skills*.
(*Checks her make-up in a compact mirror. Thinks she hears a buzzer: gets ready to go.*)
Good customer service. People-facing. I can serve a cocktail from a silver tray at thirty thousand feet without spilling a drop, disable a drunk man discreetly, calm a frightened passenger when I see that look in their eyes and never let them see that look in *my* eyes when the pilot gives us the code for *more than just turbulence keep them calm.*

VIOLET nods, as if to say: I've done exactly that.

JADE   But my airline died. Overnight. Literally. And I could have just sat around and worried about when flying would start again but that's not me.

Sprays her hair, checks her make up AGAIN in the mirror. A buzzer goes off insistently.

JADE　　I'm a doer. A positive person. Always have been. Now, everything is ... different.
Now, I serve tea in the nicest cup I can find.

DOLLY sits up and demonstrates, as if to say: I serve them tea, I never spill a drop.

JADE　　I listen more. Much more.

JADE fetches and tends alternately to someone in a wheelchair, JUNE, and someone else, GRANDA, who is just sitting like a stone.

JADE　　Sometimes, I just sit in silence, holding someone's hand, or not holding their hand, whatever *they* want.

JADE strokes GRANDA's hand gently. He doesn't acknowledge her.

JADE　　I'm learning to know when to speak
and when to let them take as long as they need to find the lost words.
Sometimes they... never find them. That's okay.

JADE waits for GRANDA to speak but it never happens.

JADE　　I'm learning to walk slowly down a corridor that must seem endless, holding someone's arm gently so I don't bruise them or let them bump into anything. Just like the aisle of a plane really... (*JADE does what she says in the following lines, alternating between GRANDA and JUNE.*) Softly folding someone's legs onto the footholds of a wheelchair and opening a door to sweet, soft fresh air. That's something I never get tired of. I couldn't do that at thirty thousand feet.

Getting used to the pace, that's taken me a while... slowing everything right down. There aren't many clocks in here, because time doesn't have much meaning.

CONSTANCE nods: there are no clocks in here. They don't want us to know how much time has passed.

JADE   Before, it was all about takeoff and schedules and fighting to *not* have to sit in the Sharon Stone jumpseat... (*She demonstrates.*) ... then fifteen minutes into being airborne, get the trolley ready. Get the napkins out. Make sure the seatbelt signs have gone off and then up and at 'em with the lunch choices.

In here, we're supposed to be spooning food into mouths by 11.30am.

She looks at the clock and tries to feed GRANDA very carefully and considerately. He refuses.

JADE   But I let people take their time.
I won't lie. I do miss it.
I miss takeoff the most. The view from the windows. Watching the sky turn silver and black and then the burning blue...
(*JUNE turns her chair around here, helped by JADE.*)
...and the arc of light as the plane banks...
But this... now. What I am now. This
is all *new*. And new is good!

She turns JUNE's chair to face the sun.

JADE   June's ninety-two today. Very upright, still beautiful, cheekbones and eyes keen and sharp. Neat hair pulled back into a bun. (*JADE gently does JUNE's hair.*) I know how to do it now, the way she likes, so that it doesn't hurt her. I know to be careful. To *care*.

She looks at GRANDA and reluctantly, pulls her gaze away from him and back to JUNE.

JADE I sometimes wonder what's going through her head, you know…?

JUNE looks up at the sky, stills JADE's hand with slight impatience, follows the progress of the little plane intently. JADE shadows what she does, eager to see life through her eyes…

JUNE How To Fly A Plane:
You have ten minutes to learn the log book off by heart they tell me.
Ten minutes? Well, that's a full eight minutes more than I'll need, I say cos you have to show the fellas you can take the teasing, but inside I am quivering –
With excitement
With terror
With sheer joy
Don't you know there's a war on, my Commanding Officer tells me. What's that smile doing on your face? For one terrible moment I think I am in real trouble.
I hold my breath –
But then she winks at me. Because she knows, my CO, she knows how utterly marvellous this is going to be. She's like me. Or I am like her, that's why she picked me, singled me out. She made this happen, she told the Powers-that-be, women can do more than you have ever dreamed. If you let them, they will fly.
We never know until the last moment what plane we'll fly or where we're even going. It could be a Lancaster, a Spitfire, a Hurricane, a Wellington, it could be Portsmouth or Scotland or oh what does it matter –
I'll fly anything anywhere, just to be up there.

Doing my bit is what I mean of course. Because there's a war on. But still…. Something inside me is singing, singing again, and I thought that we were done with singing, in this time…

JADE touches her arm lightly.

JADE Happy birthday.

JUNE is still in her past.

JUNE I can feel my feet itching to leave the ground, my toes lifting up as if we're already off, my face turning –

JADE I got you something. Only something small, it's silly, I hope you don't…

Silence.

JADE She can do this. Not speak for ages. I can't. It's just, I thought as your visitors said they might not be able to make it today…

JUNE stills her hand, with a ssshhhh. She's watching the plane. Eventually –

JUNE I've never really cared about birthdays.

JADE Oh, I'm such an idiot…

JUNE stills her hand again.

JADE Did I do something wrong?

JUNE takes her time to compose her reply. Comes back to Now.

JUNE You are very kind, my dear, and I am very ungracious. Thank you.

JADE She can sit for hours like this. She's so still. I wish I could be more like her really. But I've never been able to just sit. That's my problem. I never stop — always taking off —

JUNE There *is* something I would like you to do for me. Please refrain from *ever* calling me dear, or love, or darlin', or God forbid, *babe*. Call me June, or Mrs Norton, or call me nothing, but I beg of you —

JADE I wouldn't dream of it, June.

They half smile at each other, a little shyly.

JADE We're not supposed to have favourites. And I don't. But... June is.. *herself.*

The plane has gone. JUNE sighs.

JADE Do you want to go in?

JUNE Not yet.

JADE She never wants to go in. Not until the very last minute.

JUNE I used to fly

JADE Everyone did.

JUNE No. I *flew*.

JADE On holiday? Before everything —

JUNE I flew Spitfires. Lancasters. Wellingtons. But the Spitfires were my favourite. They were everyone's favourite.

JADE What? But when? How? Aren't they — *(decommissioned)*

JUNE 1st of June, 1943 was the first time. My birthday. That's why I don't care for presents.

Nothing else will ever come close.
Although, thank you, for your thoughtfulness...

JADE looks at her neatly wrapped gift, tries to subtly take it back, but JUNE holds onto it superbly.

JUNE Every woman should learn how to fly.
But the men didn't really want us to.

June imitates a radio announcer.

"The menace is the woman who thinks that she ought to be flying in a high-speed bomber when she really has not the intelligence to scrub the floor of a hospital properly, or who wants to nose around as an Air Raid Warden and yet can't cook her husband's dinner..."

JUNE Who cares about cooking? This is the only recipe I care about:
Take eight girls. Call them 'The 8'. Do *not* call them 'ladies'. There's nothing ladylike about this game, not anymore. Call them the Attagirls, because it sounds catchy. It means the Air Transport Auxiliary, that's all, but it sounds like we're up and at 'em, and in a way, in a way we will be.

Clothe them in an appropriate manner at all times to fly an open cockpit plane in the dead of winter at several thousand feet. Therefore, regulation uniforms are black stockings, a pleated skirt, a smart cap. This is before someone sees sense and gives us permission to wear a fur-lined flying suit and jacket and boots, but these must be removed as soon as we exit the aircraft, or there will be *repercussions*. None of us want to take the flight jackets off *ever again*. We are from all walks of life – some not even old enough to drive cars. Socialites, factory workers, a skiing instructor, a ballet dancer, mothers, a grandmother, a stunt-pilot, mathematician, architect, typist, actress, mapmaker. All we have in common is we want to fly. I leave home at eighteen and before I know it, I'm billeted with a lovely girl. Jeanie. Just my type. Straight away we were fast friends; I knew her as well as I knew myself, it seems to me... from the moment I first saw her. Nothing changed that.

JADE Sarah and me, we trained together. Did our first flight together. Paris. We were always finding something new, together... I'd never had a friend like her before... someone I could tell everything to, someone I trusted, other than you, Granda. Someone I thought I might, even... But then we swapped flights one day. People did it all the time. She took the flight I was supposed to be on to Dubai and I –

What she means but can't say is: 'I came back and she did not.'

JUNE We're two of a kind. Before our first flight, we shake hands... (*JADE and JUNE shake hands.*) and we make each other a promise; if anything happens to one of us, the other...

JADE The other goes on. That's what we always agreed. It's the rule of the air.

JUNE The other goes on.

JADE Because we are on our own, in the end..

JUNE We are on our own! Up here... always flying alone. It's not terribly easy, because I have no radio. Just a map and a compass and my own eyes, when I can take them off the silver and the blue and the great earth laid out beneath me like a painting. That's when I see what it's all for... it's for this land, those little houses covered in ivy, that brown dog, that field of corn, that woman standing in the corner of the garden staring up at me as if she can see me, as if she can't believe her own eyes... we go over the West End of London sometimes even though strictly speaking... oh, there's nothing like it, nothing on earth!

VIOLET looking up at the skies... DOLLY waving from somewhere...

JUNE Jeannie's the same. Sometimes we take off from the same airfield, same time, different planes, and we try to beat each other's takeoff time. I'd see her, grey eyes gleaming, huge grin on her lovely face. Thumbs up and away we go, spiralling off into the blue... or the grey... see you back at base...
I never want to come down. The flights are always too short for me...
I think I am wicked, because I never want the war to end. I want to go on flying, you see...
But one day I get back from my flight and the CO on duty that day says to me, without any preliminaries: 'I'm awfully sorry to tell you, your friend Jones was killed this afternoon'.
Jeannie. He means *Jeannie.*
He looks away.

JADE The plane to Dubai has been... cancelled. They tell me when we're still en route to Lagos. It wasn't cancelled. It didn't – land.

JUNE All of ten minutes later he says:
'Look. We're all very sorry, but pull yourself together, you know, there is a war on, and we have a job to do'.

JADE So when we landed, I put my face on. And my heels. And I smiled at each passenger as they disembarked because – (*She tries to compose herself.*) because no matter what, the other goes on.

JUNE   Don't look down, don't look back. Eyes right ahead and keep straight on. Look... in the direction you want to go.

JADE   Do you want to go in?

JUNE   Not yet.

JADE   We sit for hours outside most evenings. I can tell she doesn't want to go back in there... She wants to be up there, freewheeling. Not watching Flog It... Sell It... Dine It... *She flew Spitfires!* She knows what I used to – be. What I was, then. She knows I flew.

JUNE   Don't you miss it? Being up there?

JADE   No. No! I'm earthbound now. Landside. I love my job. Do *you* miss it?

Silence.

JADE   Are you cold?

JUNE   Always.

JADE wraps a blanket around JUNE, neatly, carefully, without fuss.

JADE   Shall we go in?

JUNE   No. Not yet. Not until we have to.

JADE   We look up at the sky, now turning bluish black. There's a star, just one.

JUNE   North star. My guiding light. The one faithful star that never seemed to disappear. That was how I knew where to go when it started to get dark and I was still up there. Alone, always alone, just me and the birds.

JUNE picks up the gift.

JADE I just thought… June, I just thought you might like these because…

JUNE Did you want to remain a stewardess all your life?

JADE I was actually assistant head of cabin crew but –

JUNE Never mind about serving people drinks. That's not what I mean.

JADE It's much more than that! There's a lot of responsibility, people to calm down and soothe, sometimes there are real emergencies – were. There *were* emergencies… And the stories people told me when they were frightened, or worried about something. I wasn't just a sky servant…

JUNE I mean did you never want to fly the damn plane yourself?

JADE stares at her…

JADE I – don't know… Nobody ever asked me to.

JUNE You don't wait to be asked.

Then: GRANDA and little JADE looking at the sky:

GRANDA What you looking at, chickie-dee?

JADE Look at that plane, Granda! Who do you think is flying it?

GRANDA You, my ducky egg. You're up there, in the sky…

He waves.

GRANDA I see you…

JADE   You could see my dreams, Granda. Sometimes you were in them. You still are.

Now: Jade is back with June:

JADE   I can take them back home, it's silly, I shouldn't have... I just thought, you like to sit out here so much and...

JUNE holds them out to her and gestures to her own eyes which she closes, in preparation.

JADE gently puts the aviator shades on JUNE. JUNE turns her head about, testing them out. Looks up and out at the stars and the sky.

JUNE   My dear, they're perfect. How could you possibly –?

June is back in her past.

JUNE   The Spitfire was named by the builder after his daughter, Ann, who he said was a '*proper little spitfire.*' Good for her. They also call it the *Ladies Plane* because – wait for this – it's light to the touch and incredibly sens-itive so I get into it expecting a calm gentle ride when – Oh my CHRIST it feels like a donkey's kicked me in the arse and the next thing I know I'm at a thousand feet – up with the screaming wind like a blade through me and I think *I'm* screaming but then I realise I'm singing, singing for my life, the tears whipped out of me and freezing on the wind and only the clouds and the silver sky can hear me. I have slipped the surly bonds of Earth

JADE joins in- she knows it too. Does GRANDA join in too, unheard by both of them?

JADE   And danced the skies on laughter-silvered wings...

JUNE is surprised. Carries on:

JUNE   ... and done a hundred things

JADE   You have not dreamed of...

JUNE   ... wheeled and soared and swung.

JADE   High in the sunlit silence. Hov'ring there,

JUNE   I've chased the shouting wind along, and flung...

JADE   My eager craft through footless halls of air...

BOTH   Up, up the long, delirious burning blue –

JUNE   How do you know that, I wonder?

JADE   My Granda used to say it to me. He liked the sound of the words...
So simple and so perfect, he said. Sometimes, you need just one thing, or one person, he'd say, to make you happy...

JUNE   And it's true... It's as if we're suspended up here, me and this beauty, this light, sensitive plane, swift and sleek as a gull, fast as a hawk. Nothing up here but me now for miles, not until the coast when I have to bank and turn ...

If I were a man I could keep on, fly right over the coast, leave England behind. I know I could do it, too, because nothing really matters anymore except being free. It's almost too late to turn as the sun hits my eyes from the reflection on the sea but just in time, at the last minute, I turn her. Gently.

We turn back, the beauty and I, and she lands as sweetly as any bird. I'll probably never see her again... you rarely get the same plane twice. But I'd remember that one anyway, you don't forget the ones you love, the fast and furious ones. I never want to fly anything else again after that…

As I walk away from her, I hear one of the ground crew say, 'Lads, where's the pilot?'

They're looking all over the plane, even in the footwell.

JADE I can feel my heart beating extra fast as if I'm up there with her now –

JUNE Nothing would have stopped me. *Nothing on earth.*

Back in the Now:

JADE It's not that simple…

JUNE How old are you? Twenty-seven, twenty-eight?

JADE I'm thirty. Saying it loud scares me. I've done so little, and she's done *so much* –

JUNE Oh for goodness sake, you can do whatever you want to, you girls. So what's stopping you?

JADE I'm grounded now, June. Everything's different, isn't it? This is better. Now. *Now* is better.

JUNE Why did you leave the air?

JADE I didn't leave it. It left me. My airline went bust. The world changed overnight, remember?

JUNE You could have found another airline. People will always need to fly.

JADE I had – personal responsibilities.

JUNE What was your grandfather's name?

JADE Granda. He was just always, Granda.

JUNE Was it William?

JADE nods. She's choked up.

JUNE Rather well-dressed? A bow-tie sometimes…?

JADE nods.

JUNE Beautiful manners?

GRANDA bows or does something else elegantly.

JADE nods.

JUNE Although he often seemed to – forgive me – mangle proverbs… Was that… some form of dementia?

JADE half laughs, stumbles over her words…

JADE No, he was always like that…

GRANDA from Then:

GRANDA Lovey, it's like I always say, half a horse is better than none.

JADE What can you do with half a horse?

GRANDA Well, you can't ride it very far –

JADE I need some advice, Granda.

GRANDA A word in the hand is worth two in a bush –

JADE Not everything can be solved with a dodgy proverb –

GRANDA Don't teach your Granda to suck eggs –

JADE What does that one mean? Granda! I don't know whether to stay or go –

GRANDA East, west, home's best but when you want to stay, that is when you should probably go…

JADE comes back to the Now. Sobs but tries to swallow it. Gets up...

JADE   We should probably go. Go in now.

JUNE studies her.

JUNE   His room was opposite mine, wasn't it?

JADE nods.

JUNE   I used to see you, outside. You didn't always go in... Why?

JADE   It's getting late, you know? Don't want you to catch cold.

JUNE waits.. and waits... JADE sighs. She can't outlast JUNE.

JADE   He wouldn't let me look after him. Near... near the end. Because he knew... he knew something wasn't right, in his head. Something was very wrong. He didn't want me to see what would happen – how it would happen – how he would change...

So he came here. He wanted – he *chose* this place. He interviewed five different places! He chose this one because... because it was furthest from me. He came here to be alone, to... He wouldn't let me... he... so I ... So I came here, too, anyway. Whether he liked it or not. I got a job here. It wasn't up to him!

GRANDA   You have to live your life now, chickie-dee, not mine...

JADE   But you can't just stop loving someone! It doesn't work like that...

JUNE talks directly to us, now, as GRANDA appears.

He's a bit confused.

JUNE   I'd see her often, all made up, beautifully presented, smile intact as if she was about to serve drinks at thirty thousand feet, standing outside his door. I worried a bit at first. Why didn't anyone send her away? What was she *doing* just standing there?

I'd see him come out of the room in his bow-tie, and his ironed shirt, and he always made a very slight bow to me if he caught my eye. And he *did* catch my eye.

GRANDA bows to JUNE. He winks at JADE.

GRANDA   That is a fine-looking woman you know...

JADE   Oh Granda, you're terrible.

GRANDA   A *fine* looking woman. Are you the new girl?

JADE   Granda, it's me -

GRANDA   Yes, lovey, it's you. And you are...

He reads her name tag.

GRANDA   'Jade'. What a lovely name.

Beat. JADE takes this in; the first time it's happened...

JADE   It didn't matter if he didn't always know me. It *didn't matter*. I was still there, near him. Watching out for him. Because sometimes... that's all you can do for someone you love. Make sure the chef knows that he likes fish pie with hot sauce. Slip into his room and switch the Aldi teabags for Yorkshire Gold. Tell his Alexa to play Al Green on shuffle instead of Radio 2 which he shouted at impatiently. Just stay as close as I could for as long as I can. So... the need to... fly... didn't come *close*.

JUNE   I told my son and his wife when I came here: Don't visit me. Don't bring the outside in to me.

Say goodbye and don't come back. Sometimes we have to be cruel. But they wouldn't listen either...

JUNE wheels herself off quietly as JADE reminisces...

JADE He gave up his life to look after me! He had his own shop, he loved that shop... he could have said no when my mum – when mum couldn't –

JADE can't let herself go down that path though.

JADE I mean he could have gone round the world, met someone lovely after Gran died, done anything but he stayed. He stayed *for me,* when no one else did ... he laughed at my stupid jokes, he put his hands on my forehead and cooled me down when I was ill... he had very cool hands, great at pastry. He drew pictures with me. Awful pictures! He picked me up from school every day, the teachers all loved him, he never ever let me down not once every reading time every school play every everything.

When I passed my airside exam he was there waving my first flight off. Every time I flew I saw his face in my mind, I looked out of the window and I saw him smiling up at me as we taxi'd along the runway, no matter where it was in the world. I saw him in old men in Grenada, in bars in Ireland, lining the street in Bulgaria, on the beach in Sydney. I heard his soft voice in Singapore, in Marseille I smelled his talcum powder and pipe tobacco, in Lagos I heard his rumbling laugh. And now... I can't leave here. How can I leave here? This is the last place he ever was on this earth and now there's nothing on earth left without him.

The women re-group: VIOLET, DOLLY and CONSTANCE.

VIOLET S*he's* the One?

CONSTANCE She's lovely –

DOLLY She's lonely –

VIOLET Too much make up and where's her rifle?

CONSTANCE When I was her age, I was restless...

VIOLET She needs a kick up the arse -

CONSTANCE She needs hope -

DOLLY She needs *us*.

CONSTANCE We were lucky really... we had each other...

VIOLET I made my own luck. I needed no one. She's *not* the One –

CONSTANCE But she could be –

VIOLET We need someone of courage, someone made of steel and heart and fire, not this... over made-up floozy!

CONSTANCE Nobody is what they seem, though...

DOLLY Someone once asked me, aren't you scared to go up into the sky? A little slip of a thing like you? You'll blow away! But they didn't see what I had inside me... It only takes one person to see what you really are.

VIOLET Reel her in then.

JADE June asks me to take her to Mrs Shepherd's room. This is unusual because June doesn't really talk to anybody in here... I think she's a bit bored with them all if I'm honest... stuck in front of the TV. *Deal It... Flog It... Dine It... always* on.

JUNE Here we are.

JADE wheels JUNE to a door and knocks.

JADE I don't think I've met Mrs Shepherd? I didn't think there were any rooms on this floor...

JUNE You go in first, dear. You'll like her.

JADE Oh, I never go in without permission... I never forget this is somebody's home.

But JUNE gently pushes her in. The room is unlike any regular care home room, precisely because it is

not real. It must look and feel off somehow, but in an enticing way...

DOLLY is pulling an apron on. She prepares serving tea to the (imaginary?) audience.

JADE Mrs Shepherd?

DOLLY Tea, madam?

JADE Oh no, I've brought June to see you...?

DOLLY Another cup, sir? Are the sugar tongs shiny enough for you, my lady?

Spits on them discreetly, winks at JADE then polishes.

JADE Is she... *alright?* Only June is waiting outside and –

JADE looks back outside but there is no one...

JADE June...?

DOLLY is quite loud, JADE hastily goes back in.

DOLLY Bored, bored, sooooo bored, only another *seven* hours to go, then another tomorrow then the same the next day probably until I DIE but as my mother says, Alexandra Palace is a very respectable place for a girl of my age... More hot water, sir, of course. Sorry madam, we've run out of Darjeeling, then a man with a louder voice than most, a real complainer, here we go, what have I done wrong now?

While MONSIEUR berates his lot, DOLLY polishes everything she can so she can get closer and listen: maybe even a bald head in the audience or JADE's watch.

MONSIEUR Two hours to go til the show starts and *no girl* – there are plenty of girls – girls are ten-a-penny but not girls like my wife, not girls who will let you shoot a gun at an egg on the top of her head and trust you not to miss but the truth is, I may have *slightly* grazed her *un peu* hence the bleeding … Where is the one that will trust you with her life? The one that has *courage*, will hold her head up and look the audience in the eyes and smile while *BOOM*! I have made a terrible *leetle* mistake and now there can be no show because no girl will go on in her place…

DOLLY I WILL! *To us* (did I shout that out loud?)

MONSIEUR We don't need any more tea.

DOLLY I will be that girl, sir!

MONSIEUR Do you usually listen to customers conversations?

DOLLY I can do it! Sir… When he stops laughing, he looks me up and down as if he's measuring me for a coffin.

MONSIEUR What's your name, girl?

DOLLY Elizabeth. Sir.

MONSIEUR That's not the right name for this sort of thing. Don't waste my time. *L'addition, s'il vous plait*…

He clicks his fingers imperiously.

DOLLY – but they call me Dolly, sir. Dolly Shepherd!

MONSIEUR And why do they call you that?

DOLLY When I was born, my grandmother said: oh, she's such a little thing, she's just a dolly. But, I'm stronger than I look. I'm sixteen, sir, but, I'm very mature.

MONSIEUR Well, *Dollee,* I am looking for a girl to have an egg shot off the top of her head. With a gun. Bang! Do you like the sound of that?

DOLLY I do, sir.

MONSIEUR Why?

DOLLY My job is very boring. I think nothing'll ever happen to me ever again in my entire life if I stay here much longer, so just give me a chance. Please... Sir.

He walks all around her, staring at her, deliberately intimidating her. Too close, then sudden movements, then too close.

MONSIEUR Can you keep very still, Dolly Shepherd? Can you keep very still as if your entire life depended on it? Because... It will.

DOLLY turns to JADE.

DOLLY Load me up. Carefully. But quick!

She gestures. JADE haphardly seizes a tea tray, loads it, puts it on DOLLY's head and as he watches, gestures to JADE to hand her piece after piece of china which she loads onto the tray. JADE helps her balance.

DOLLY More...

MONSIEUR *Non!*

DOLLY   More...

MONSIEUR *Ça suffit–*

She silences him and the others in the tearoom (*audience)- ssshhhh!

DOLLY   I can do it. I can do it!

She balances perfectly as he walks around her.

DOLLY   Yes sir. I can keep very, very still.

MONSIEUR Alright, Dolly Shepherd!

He gestures to Jade to put an egg on Dolly's head.

He prepares himself.

MONSIEUR Drum roll please. Close your eyes

JADE makes a drum roll. She's a great sidekick.

DOLLY   Oh, I don't need to...

MONSIEUR It's not for your sake, you little fool! It's for mine. Close your eyes!

DOLLY   I can't.

He gestures to someone in the crowd. They put a blindfold on him.

DOLLY   They never told me about this part!

MONSIEUR It's more theatrical like this... Monsieur likes a challenge. Now, hold your breath – and, Dolly Shepherd –

DOLLY   Sir?

MONSIEUR If you can do this – IF you can do this... Next time, you can go up up in the air!

He shoots. An egg shatters loudly.

DOLLY opens her eyes, wipes her face, smiles like the world is hers.

MONSIEUR Welcome to your new life, Dolly Shepherd!

Applause from JADE and MONSIEUR disappears like magic.

DOLLY But I am not Dolly Shepherd any more. I am the girl who was shot at and survived and smiled when the egg ran down her face.

DOLLY bows. First to JADE, then to the audience.

DOLLY Time to go up.

JADE I'm not sure what's happening. A man who is not here anymore just shot a woman who is here who seems to live here who looks like a teenager who seems happy that a man just shot at her head and now –

DOLLY – now I go home and tell my beloved aunty what I'm going to do. I am bubbling with excitement, I can't keep still... Guess what, Aunty? I'm going to make a parachute descent in my bloomers! (*DOLLY puts them on.*) I expect her to be as excited as I am, but....

AUNTY is shrouded in huge black feathers and wearing a hat and is very, very imperious (a bit Lady Bracknell):

AUNTY If.... You. Go. Ahead with such an entirely preposterous idea, you will. Never. Enter my house again.

DOLLY She means it. And... I'm very fond of her. She's taken me in, given me a job in her maribou feather shop, lets me live with her, and, I am the one who looks after her, who dresses her ulcerated leg every day.

DOLLY tries to make her decision.

DOLLY But... to fly... to have the chance... it might never come again... not like this...

DOLLY decisively starts rolling bandages up.

DOLLY There are two days to go before the jump. I buy a stock of lotions. One day to go. (*DOLLY tries to get AUNTY to look at her*) Aunty... Aunty... Aunty!

AUNTY utterly refuses to look at her. DOLLY turns around her until she has her in a contorted position where she can't avoid it.

DOLLY Aunty! I know you're not speaking to me but I wanted to let you know there are enough dressings and lotions and bandages here for three months.

AUNTY What on earth for?

DOLLY I'm going to make my first parachute jump tomorrow and you told me

BOTH – if you do this disgraceful thing you will never enter my house again...

DOLLY So I've prepared a good supply for you to dress your leg yourself in future. Because... I am going.

DOLLY holds AUNTY, forcing her to look her in the eyes.

DOLLY I am going – up! Up there! (*DOLLY gently tilts AUNTY's head up.*) Look... look at all that sky...

DOLLY holds her so tight it's as if they are fighting to the death.

DOLLY I can't help it. I'm sorry... I have to go!

Standoff. DOLLY lets her go.

They stare at each other.

AUNTY Don't *ever* tell me about it. You can go – up. But you must never, ever talk to me about it. Promise. I couldn't stand it!

DOLLY So you see I have no one. No one that I can tell. No one...

JADE No one I can tell things to, but you... (*Berates herself for using present tense*) – *could* tell. *Could*. Granda, you'd be amazed at what's going on in here –

DOLLY Starting final checks.

DOLLY briskly sets about getting the hot air balloon ready for takeoff, making JADE help her.

DOLLY Rope. Check?

JADE I thought it was just the usual *Crafternoon* with felt-making and crochet which obviously you hated...

DOLLY Compass. Check!

JADE ... even the word *Crafternoon* made you snort with rage *it's not even a word* but –

DOLLY Sanitary towel. Check!

JADE picks up a massive sanitary towel belt with awe.

DOLLY Dead rose from over-enthusiastic admirer? Check.

JADE examines it with slight disgust.

DOLLY Lucky charm. Check. Mirror? Check. That's it.

JADE This is getting out of control...

She finds a duck.

JADE   You'd think I was imagining things...

DOLLY throws the duck out.

DOLLY   Flew too close. Burned to death. Ready for takeoff. Pull the ropes in.

The balloon is fired beneath them with a WHOOMPH.

JADE   What was that –?

JADE tries to climb out. DOLLY pulls her back in.

DOLLY   What are you doing? Pull the ropes in! NOW!

JADE pulls the ropes in without thinking. DOLLY shouts.

DOLLY   AND... LET GO!

JADE tries to get out, DOLLY pulls her back in and they collapse together.

DOLLY   Careful! you'll unbalance Hetty.

JADE   Who's Hetty?

DOLLY   The balloon of course. Good girl, Hetty! I didn't know that she was my destiny until she happened to me. Sometimes life's like that – pfff! Up you go! Seize it, I told myself, pull the cord and –

They take off.

JADE   Wooooaaaahhhhhh! is this thing even legal?

DOLLY   Stay STILL –

JADE   Who ARE you?

DOLLY   Fifteen, twenty, Dolly Shepherd at your service, twenty-five, thirty...

JADE   I want to get out!

DOLLY Fifty-five, seventy, hundred and thirty, that's good – what are you doing?

JADE Make it STOP!

DOLLY I thought you were a skyflyer?

JADE is trying to climb out.

JADE There's no seat belts! There's no SEATS!

DOLLY We're not high enough yet to descend. STAY STILL!

JADE stays still. Looks down.

JADE ARRGHHHHH! We're so high!

DOLLY Not high enough yet.

JADE They say don't look down – but look at all the people! You can really see them...

DOLLY Yes, there's always a crowd waiting to see us fall... that's why we have the parachutes check.

JADE WHAT?

DOLLY The chutes! Get them! NOW! CHECK!

DOLLY grabs the chutes and thrusts them at JADE.

JADE Oh no I'm NOT –

DOLLY Oh yes, you are. Weather conditions are perfect. And besides, there's only one way down from here –

JADE You're trained, tell me you're trained in this!

DOLLY Oh yes, fully trained. I've had a whole half an hour.

JADE And you haven't had any accidents, tell me you haven't? *Half an hour?* I had eighteen months training after I'd fought off fourteen thousand applicants.

They're floating...

DOLLY So you see I have no one. No one that I can tell.

JADE No one...

DOLLY Not a soul knows what it feels like –

JADE No one knows what it's like

DOLLY To be lifted into the air as though by a giant hand...

JADE To have the person you love, the only person –

DOLLY To have no control!

JADE Float away from you...

DOLLY Float into the air

JADE Can't find them...

DOLLY I wriggle my feet and laugh. I am walking on air. I am walking on air! Above my head the canopy opens and billows softly as if it is breathing... as though, like me, it is glad to be alive... the dearest friend I have in the world. The sounds of the crowds, the barking of dogs, even birdsong all disappears as I soar higher and higher. I am too high for the birds.

JADE/DOLLY Just me, free

JADE Freefalling

DOLLY Alone

JADE	Alone
DOLLY	Going higher and higher
JADE	To take off, to feel the thrust of the engines
DOLLY	To have no control!
JADE	To suddenly lift up up and away
DOLLY	Float into the air
JADE	Going higher and higher, out of control
DOLLY	Too high, too soon... it's time to go down, but the chute won't open. It won't open!
BOTH	I tell myself that I just have to hold on because it's unthinkable to let go...
DOLLY	I'm high... higher, much higher than I ever have before, higher than I should, but I can't stop. Clouds swaddle me, cold and moist. And then I'm above the clouds – oh! 'You'll do this once too often' they said... maybe they were right! Cold... so cold... I'll fall... I must hold on. Keep my senses.
BOTH	Stay awake...
DOLLY	Sing... SING that song, the one that father used to sing to get him through bad times –

DOLLY sings.

DOLLY	There is a happy land, come come away
JADE	There is a happy land
BOTH	– far, far away...

As they sing, GRANDA joins in from wherever he is, probably Then.

JADE   Granda used to sing that to me when I couldn't sleep.

DOLLY   The ground rushes up to me now too fast TOO FAST! Hold on!

DOLLY falls suddenly, GRANDA falls in Then. JADE reacts.

DOLLY   I have the strangest sensation in my legs, as if they are being stabbed by tiny needles. Don't touch me. Don't try to – move me. So much – pain... Don't... Just let me lie here...

DOCTOR   There is no doubt that everybody admires the pluck of the brave girl who found herself in such difficulties in mid-air, but Miss Dolly Shepherd will never walk again as a result of her terrible injuries...

JADE   Wait – what?

DOCTOR   And this is why public opinion should put an end to parachute descents by females...

DOLLY   Never walk again they say, well –

DOCTOR   The best thing is to find a place for you in a hospital for incurables.

DOLLY   I *will* walk again...

GRANDA   The best thing is if I find me a nice place, my honey pie, where they can care for me...

JADE   I can care for you!

GRANDA   But two roads are better than one... no, that's not it... Two roads diverge... Three heads are better than one... no, that's not –

JADE has a moment of clarity:

JADE I've only just realised why all his proverbs sound so... off... It's because he is... He's...*off*. It's as if he's left, already. He's nothing on earth anymore, he's up up and away... Not himself... But if he's not himself, then who is he?

She shakes herself back to the matter in hand.

GRANDA All water off the back of the duck – no...

JADE It doesn't matter, Granda. I can look after you better than anyone else, you know I can.

GRANDA I don't fucking want you to!

Silence. He looks at her, helplessly.

GRANDA I don't want you to...

JADE I'll never leave you. You're my everything, remember?

GRANDA Always and everything, my apple-pie. Where am I?

JADE You're here with me, Granda.

GRANDA I'm home. It was a trick question. And home is where the heart is, dear love, as I keep telling you. And you're always here – But, you see, you shouldn't be. Go out there! Go out there and live.

He gives JADE a stone.

JADE What's this, Granda?

GRANDA Don't you remember?

JADE Remember what?

GRANDA Which one of us is forgetting things now? Take it, honey-pie... Keep it always with you. Keep it close to you... It means the world to me. Take it wherever you go. Until you don't need it anymore...

DOLLY   When the doctor says, '*I'm afraid you won't walk again.*' I don't believe him. Of course I will. '*It's one of the hazards of such extremely risky hobbies, I'm afraid. Flying is not a suitable occupation for a young lady and now look at you.*' Yes *now* look at me. Now help me. Help me stand, take my weight –

JADE helps DOLLY.

DOLLY   – because I will walk again, and what's more I'll go up again and again and higher and higher.

They're up in the air without JADE realising.

JADE   Why would you risk it when you know what could happen? You know what could go wrong, you could get caught in a tree and break your neck, land on the ground like a... like a stone... break your heart into a thousand tiny pieces... why would you do it?

She gets the stone out and looks at it.

DOLLY   What's all this life we've got in us for, then? Why waste it?

DOLLY peers over the edge, perks up.

DOLLY   Look where we are.

JADE   They say don't look down.

DOLLY   I say look down. There!

JADE   An ugly building... could be anywhere...

DOLLY   Look! we're over north London, right above Holloway prison. Look!

JADE But it's been knocked down – it doesn't exist…

DOLLY What do you see? What do your eyes tell you? LOOK! That's where they keep the suffragettes.

DOLLY leans out, makes a raised fist of support. CONSTANCE waves up at them.

DOLLY NO SURRENDER! But that's not where we're going. West! *(She swerves.)* You're lucky. Weather conditions are perfect, luckily, because there's only one way down from here… Time to let go!

JADE No – no – I can't! I'm not ready!

DOLLY Oh darling, we're never ready. We have to go when the wind takes us. You're not meant to be earthbound, you never will be.

JADE I can't do it – how can I do it?

DOLLY It's time.

DOLLY throws the stone out.

JADE NOOOOO!

DOLLY Only one way to get it. Follow it down.

DOLLY pushes her out.

JADE Oooooooooooh… Oh, it's… Oh, it's floating and falling and falling and floating and terrifying don't look down I want to look down I don't want to I DO look I'm looking! Granda if you could see me if you could see THIS look at all the trees and the people and that very small brown dog and JESUS the power lines and birds and a fox and a bin and the ground rushing up –

DOLLY Good luck –

JADE – and the ground rushing up – where are you going?

DOLLY Wherever the wind takes me –

JADE Dolly! Don't leave me!

DOLLY I've a feeling you'll be fine…

JADE No, you don't understand, I can't… I've got to get back, June needs me – ohhhhhh… I'm flying I'm FLYING again I'm falling I'M FALLING! You never told me how to FALL!

DOLLY Just bend your knees and bounce when you hit the ground and then lightly onto your back and roll over… But the main thing to remember, the most important thing to remember is –

And she's gone.

JADE What? WHAT?

Is there the sound of laughter? JADE is in freefall.

JADE – but how will I know where to land? Somebody! Help me! I don't know where I am…

GRANDA Take your chances, chucky egg. Take your chances when they come because chance is like a bird…

JADE What? How is chance like a bird?

GRANDA It can fly away in a moment, roll off your back like a duck…

JADE I don't know how to land…

GRANDA You will land in the right place lovely, you will land where you are meant to be…

JADE I don't know where I'm meant to be!

GRANDA Don't bite the hand that lays the golden egg. Where do you *want* to be?

JADE With you. Little and safe and just with you.

GRANDA Then let the wind take you where it will. I'll make you a bet, my darling girl, you will land where you need to be.

As GRANDA counts down, a room buzzer starts going insistently.

GRANDA Five...

JADE I don't know what to do without you

GRANDA Four. Do you trust me?

JADE You never let me down once

GRANDA Three. Then turn your face towards the west and smile, smile, smile two, one...

JADE lands and finds the room that's been buzzing. She knocks.

JADE Er – hello? You were buzzing?

MAY opens the door. It is Now. Full of smiles and energy, full of chatter.

MAY Do you know what they did?

JADE Sometimes people think they're talking to someone from the past... you get used to it... No, what did they do?

MAY They only went and made a bet didn't they?

MAY is rolling up her sleeves. She smiles at JADE, beckons her closer as if she's got a secret or a great big joke.

MAY They bet us that we can't build a plane. A Wellington. Not just any plane, a bloody great bomber.

But not just build it! Build it in thirty hours from start to take-off, that's why they said we'll never do it.
Do you think we *can* do it? Well?

JADE   Where do you think you are?

MAY   Welsh Wales love. They round up all the women and the invalids and the old men, all the ones *no use* for the war. Nothing makes me madder than being told I'm no use. So I say, alright, I'll give it a go. Because there's a war on and because…

To be honest… because it's a lot more exciting than my job at the Co-op. Bored to death I am do you know what I mean? So they get us girls in, a lot of us aren't girls no more either, and I didn't know one end of a screwdriver from another back then. I do now. Built of steel, me, after that. (*She goes back into her past.*) My mam, she says, '*I don't want you doing that. It's not right, it's not a job for women, what about the kiddies*'?

Yeh. I look her in the eye and I say, mam. There's a war on. Imagine… just imagine, looking up at the skies and seeing a plane going off to fight them bastards, them bastards that took George and knowing that I made that plane… I helped make it.

Or… imagine looking up at the empty skies and thinking, well, I could have helped make it, but my OWN MAM wouldn't look after HER OWN GRANDKIDS.

She shuts her gob then.

Me, I don't sleep for three days beforehand, I'm that worried – how can we do it?

We're taken into the aircraft hanger and we look at these enormous things, these – beasts, and I think, there's no way on earth – *nothing on earth* is going to make this happen in time, in thirty hours.

They sit us in rows like naughty kids in school, giggling a bit cos... How can *we* build a plane? and then...

They bring in this MASSIVE clock on a stand.

And they set it. They set the timer!

'Nothing much at stake, girls', our gaffer says, 'only national pride and winning the war and avenging our own people oh and showing those who think they're better than us what women and *in-valids* can do. Shall we show them or shall we go home, eh?' I stop giggling then. She's bloody right.

We're off.

We stitch the linen carapace – eight stitches to the inch, or the wind could get it and rip the seams open.

We drive the roof cranes that shift the wings and tail fins into position.

We install the electrics and yeh, I do part of that. Me! That couldn't change a lightbulb!

And now – I can start to see the skeleton of this great creature that's going to lift off. Go up there? Into all that.... Nothingness... up there? It's impossible. We'll never do it. It'll never lift off, surely –

I've never been in a plane, none of us have, it's not something we'll ever do, we're just ordinary people. This is the closest I'll ever get.

MAY beckons to JADE to join her... she takes JADE's hand and together...

They step inside. Echoes...

MAY   So just for one sneaky minute, I step inside the belly of the beast. It's like being inside a whale, or a dinosaur, or something in a dream or a nightmare, all ribs and wire and wind screaming in and out of the yawning gaps.

This soundscape foreshadows the hellish prison sounds... and also reminds JADE of the care home when she first goes in...

JADE remembers standing outside GRANDA's room in the care home.

JADE I can hear you breathe, Granda... Hear the click as you set your glasses down. In a minute you'll forget where you've put them and ask where they are... or knock over a water glass because it's not in the right place. Not where I'd put it. I can't leave you here Granda... I can't do it!

MAY We can't do it. We'll never do it. I want to run back home and say *mam, mam, you were right, now hand over my kids and forget it ever happened* –

They both want to turn tail... but...

JADE But –?

MAY But... I think of my George and how he said to me, before he went, that last time; 'if anything happens to me...'

BOTH *'You go on'.*

MAY And something inside me starts to rage and simmer and settle and click, just like the gears and the workings of the big beast. We can do this.

The clock's ticking down now. We swarm to slot together its body, to assemble the engine, to tightly sew its fabric shell. We work like one seething mass. We fit the propellers to the wings. It's coming together so fast, we start laying bets on whether we'll beat our target. Oh I'd bloody love that!

'Can you work through the night', the gaffer asks us, she says; 'would your fella mind if he could see you now?'

He'd be proud, says I – (*Lifts her chin with defiance*) Cos I'm going *nowhere* until this is done. None of us are. Nothing could stop us, nothing would make me go home, I don't care how tired I am. For it's flying we are now, the speed we work at, our fingers over the fabric, over the steel, in formation, high as kites. I'm only five foot two but I'll always be sky-tall as this plane, now.

In them last long hours, we stretch the Irish linen that we've bloodied our hands sewing and we give the beast its clothes, for its journeys, for maybe only one journey ever, who knows? And while we do it, while we make the plane ready, we sing, us girls and *in-valids* and old men and those who are *no use,* we sing and we sew and we stretch and we sing our words into the beast

(GRANDA and JUNE might sing along too... same era...)

so it may be lucky, so it may go safe, so it may stay safe for whoever flies it. and one last thing... for luck, we etch a secret word inside the cockpit. That was *my* idea that was.

We wait until the pilot gets into it. Covered in their overalls and helmet and goggles, they don't even look human, but they put their thumb up to us when they're sat in our cockpit. Our cockpit that we made with our red raw hands.

Work has progressed so fast the pilot has had to be woken from slumber for the maiden flight.

JUNE, in aviation gear, yawning, putting her hat on.

JUNE   I hope to God they haven't missed anything. I'm so tired. And it's my first time in a Wellington.

MAY shouts at the pilot as she takes off...

MAY Listen you! We was bet we'd never build a bomber in thirty hours. We didn't do it in thirty hours. We did it in twenty-four hours and forty-eight minutes! I never knew who flew it, our Beast... never knew their name... (*May comes back to the present: Now:*)
I'd like to have known...
If they slipped the surly bonds of earth
And danced the skies on silvered wings one more time.
I'd just... like to know.
But I tell you one thing...
There's no going back to the Co-op now, not after this. Not ever.

JADE But I can tell you who she was! I know her! It was June – !

But MAY has disappeared, leaving only the sound of her slightly raucous, raunchy laughter in the air...

JADE Granda, you wouldn't believe what I just saw happen – a woman I know now just took off in a plane, then made by a woman who couldn't change a lightbulb, oh I don't know why I talk to you like this. As if you're still here. Must stop. Must STOP.

JADE hits herself in the head, trying to beat some sense into herself. GRANDA gently stops her.

GRANDA Love never dies, my angel, it just passes to another person but you never know who... it can come without warning from anywhere... Remember when your mum brought you to me?

JADE doesn't want to remember this, though. It hurts. Then... whispers...

GRANDA You're such a little thing, when you first come to me... you love to play hide and seek... It's the only game you like… I don't know why… and you always hide in the same place… You want me to find you, to know I'll always find you. I promise I'll always find you. Now. But where am *I*, now?

JADE Hide and seek was the *only* game I knew. And… somehow, he always knew where to find me… I don't know how. It was… magic! He… was magic…

Then. JADE in GRANDA's garden, 8 years old:

GRANDA Where can she be?
Is she… in my sock drawer? No… Is she… behind my toilet? (*A Giggle.*) No! I know! She must be…

GRANDA lets JADE surprise him.

JADE Surprise! I was in the GARDEN!

GRANDA Here you are! What a clever hiding place…

JADE Look, Granda-

She gives him something.

JADE It's for you.

GRANDA But what is it, my little love?

JADE It's special. See?

They both examine it carefully.

GRANDA I do see… I'll keep it safe my chickie-dee.

He puts it close to his heart. Then into a special tin.

JADE When's mummy coming to get me?

GRANDA She's not well, my darling, so you're going to live with me for a little while.

JADE Forever?

GRANDA We don't know yet. But I'll always look after you, my little bean.

Now: Outside his room in the care home; GRANDA looks at her for a long time.

GRANDA Why are you in here?

JADE I'm your granddaughter...

GRANDA laughs gently. An alarm goes off in another room. JADE knows she should go but she's torn...

GRANDA I know that... I haven't lost my mind yet. But... Who are you *going* to be? That is the question. I'd like...

GRANDA turns to stone. An alarm goes off again.

JADE Granda? I don't know. I don't know who I'm going to be! Can't I just stay the same? Can't everything just go back to the way it always was?

JADE Granda... look at me, please just look at me. Granda? (*She brushes his hair, straightens his tie. Kisses his cheek very gently.*) That was the last time he knew who I was.

The alarm goes off again. And again.

JADE It was like he gave up. I'd hear him... crying, sometimes, very quietly.

JUNE I'd hear him, too. Do you know... Sometimes, he tried to ask the Alexa to play something–

GRANDA Alexa – play that Warm Villains one!

JUNE Of course he meant *Vaughan* Williams but instead he'd get –

JADE/JUNE *Robbie* Williams.

JUNE So... I would knock on his door, and... (*Clears her throat*) Alexa, play Vaughan Williams 'The Lark Ascending'. Please.

JUNE and GRANDA sit and listen to the first few bars of the Lark Ascending. They don't look at each other. They might not even be in the same space, (although I think they have done this same thing several times before in the same space) but they are sharing something beautiful. Meanwhile, JADE goes to answer the buzzer that's ringing on a nearby resident's door.

JUNE Who is she? The young woman who waits?

GRANDA is silent. He looks at her. It's impossible to tell what he knows or feels. He holds something out in his hand and she touches it. He tries to give it to her but she folds his hand back around it.

JADE knocks on the door. There's no answer. She gently pushes the door open.

JADE Hello? Just Jade here, I'm just checking everything's alright...? Hello...? (*She can hear strange, disturbing sounds. She's frightened.*) Is there – is there somebody in here? Are you alright? You were ringing your buzzer... I don't know what to do.

Prepare for emergency landing. Okay. Assume nothing, expect anything, brace position.

She goes in, fearfully but bravely.

JADE is in another netherworld room. The mournful sounds of The Lark Ascending merge with, discordantly, the angry, sad, scared sounds of prison life; pens and cutlery rattled furiously against barred windows, screaming, singing, laughter that's tinged with despair, crying, shouts, banging.

It's the prison cell of CONSTANCE.

JADE Hello... Hello...?

JADE is terrified when she sees a woman (CONSTANCE).

The cell door slams shut.

Blackout.

End of Act One.

ACT TWO

Constance is sitting at a table with her back to us. She appears to be writing...

CONSTANCE Just before I came here, Mama gave me a new writing desk, and told me that I must spend my time there writing letters in my *beautiful* hand to the local people of note, to – invite them to the house. She hoped that this would lead to my being –*accepted* a little more in – *society*.

But my *ventures* meet with little success as I am not very *interested* in society, Mama noted, but she wished that I would overcome this and be a good – daughter. It may however be just – a little –*late* – for that.

She turns from the table. She has been intricately carving her own skin. JADE is hypnotised by what she sees.

CONSTANCE You must be the new room mate. *(She holds her hand out formally.)* Constance. Lady Constance Lytton. Connie. Con. My family call me Con. Oh – Do not be scared... (*CONSTANCE goes towards JADE just a little.)* It is not as bad as you would think, prison. In many ways, it is just – a room of one's own. Just – *(She tries not to cry.)* Just a room, sparsely furnished –

JADE – a room in a prison.

CONSTANCE Just a room in North London.

JADE It doesn't exist anymore! Holloway prison doesn't exist!

CONSTANCE It is common to have delusions.

JADE Holloway prison has been sold off to the highest bidder.

CONSTANCE You must lay hold of your inward self, and keep tight hold.

JADE takes CONSTANCE's wrist gently and rubs her hands tenderly.

JADE You're cold –

CONSTANCE Nobody has touched me for so long a time...

JADE Your hands are so cold...

CONSTANCE My heart is not strong, you see.

CONSTANCE shows JADE her chest where she has been carving...

CONSTANCE I am writing the words "Votes for Women" on my body, with a needle. I began here – look: *(Her heart.)* And I will end it – Here. *(Her face.)*

It is the only thing I have ever done that I know to be worthwhile. The doctors try to stop me – they don't want the world to see Lady Constance Lytton carved and marked like a common woman but the last letter of my message will be visible on my cheek the day I leave here –

A great friend of mine, Mrs Pankhurst, told me only two days ago that they in power little know what women are. Women are very slow to rouse, she said, and I think this to be true, but once they are aroused, once they are determined, she said, nothing on earth and nothing in heaven will make women give way. We have to remember that. We have to keep tight hold of that.

JADE But I know that. It's a famous quote... it's –

CONSTANCE No, you misunderstand me, she said it to me only two days ago as we were brought to the cells-

JADE   It's – legend, now...

CONSTANCE But, when is this now?

JADE   I don't understand-

CONSTANCE What did you do?

JADE   I answered the/ buzzer.

CONSTANCE /I beg your pardon. I mean, what crime did you do to be in here? What are you in for as they say?

JADE   I –

She can't speak. CONSTANCE is embarrassed.

CONSTANCE I am so sorry. You don't need to tell me. I am very impolite, my Mama tells me, that is why no one will marry me. I say what is in my head and often it is too – frank. Are you married? Do you have children? Why are you wearing such strange clothes? What are you in /for?

JADE   /I left someone to die. I let the person I loved most in the world die. Alone –

Now CONSTANCE is silent. JADE is in deep despair but typically, she tries to swallow it down, not let it out.

Then. JADE visits GRANDA in his garden.

GRANDA   I don't know much about anything really, as your mum always told me... I do know that you can bury a lot of troubles in the earth but their shoots will always push through sooner or later so... Here's my advice for all it's worth, lovey.

Just close your eyes, hold tight and think of taking off...

Do you remember your first flight? You were shaking with nerves.

You can always tell your old Granda anything, you know, duck.... What's to do? I know there's something... you've always been my special girl, since you were little and you were the only one to laugh at my terrible jokes.

JADE I'm so alone, Granda... so lonely...

GRANDA Did you know, long ago, the word *alone* was two words... all one... I'll always be with you, my lamb, I told you. Always, and in all ways.

Did you understand it yet? What you have to do now?

CONSTANCE is crying.

JADE Did you know, long ago, the word alone was two words... all one...

CONSTANCE All one... I like that. Yes. I like that better.

CONSTANCE breathes deeply, calming herself.

CONSTANCE I must tell my brother that. He worries that I am too much isolated.

LORD VICTOR's letter flies into the cell or does CONSTANCE take it from a book where she has hidden it, much read and much-treasured.

VICTOR How are you, my best and dearest sister? We worry terribly about you, for we hear bad reports of ill-treatment towards women in the prison but I know you will not be conquered by this. I doubt any man could have a braver sister. I am not sure that I could bear it myself, what you are engaged upon, but then you have always been stronger and better than me, despite appearances. You are my superior in every way and I bow before you. Remember that I am with you in spirit and will do everything I can for your cause at Parliament. Above all, dearest Con, remember this; that little patch of sky that you may I hope be able to see from your cell window is the same sky that I can see, and the birds that fly above you will soon fly over us here. Your affectionate brother, Victor.

JADE He has your back.

CONSTANCE He is my – one. I believe that we only need one person who truly understands us. That is enough.

JADE But when they go...

CONSTANCE People go on. We go on. I can endure almost anything. Look for the tiny joys. You would be surprised how happy I am here... Look! (*She takes JADE to look out of her window.*) From my little window I can see my own little patch of sky. I am so rich, I think. I can see everything I cannot have. Look! Oh, look! Look at that *lovely* woman up there, so free–

JADE Dolly – it's Dolly!

They both peer out of the window and CONSTANCE waves.

CONSTANCE Do you know her? I should love to know her!

JADE Dolly! Help! Get us OUT OF HERE!

CONSTANCE Sssh- shh, they'll hear you –!

They watch through the window as DOLLY disappears from sight.

JADE She's gone – she's gone!

Suddenly a rap on the door, very sharply.

WARDER Back away from the door!

JADE Who's that?

CONSTANCE It's the warder... the unhappy one... some of them, I truly believe, dislike how they must treat us... Not all. Some just dislike us. It's because we're on hunger strike. Listen –

A strange loud almost musical sound starts.

JADE Why are they singing? What have they got to sing about?

The sound builds.

JADE It's not singing...

CONSTANCE They're forcing the tube down a woman's throat and she's – screaming. And – It's my turn next.

Footsteps get nearer.

JADE No – they won't do that to *you* –

CONSTANCE Not when I am Lady Constance Lytton? No. You are right. And so I shall not be her. Me.

Banging on the door which intensifies under the next section:

CONSTANCE Help me. Quickly! The hat. It hides my hair.

JADE passes her an old hat and helps her dress.

CONSTANCE Coat. It smells bad. That's – good. Glasses. Oh, I can hardly see. That tatty old bag, please, quickly!

Now, I am Jane Warton. I made the name up. Now I am a common woman. Now I am simply prisoner number D28686 – NOW see how they treat me. Now see what they do.

A tapping starts: No Surrender.

CONSTANCE taps back.

And back: No Surrender

A chant starts, soft and low and firm, until there's a whole prison full of taps and screams and growing chants: No surrender. It makes JADE fearful and excited.

CONSTANCE I'll never be alone again. Wherever I am in the world, no matter how far into the future, I will hear this, this – love – and I will know that in my worst moments, someone is with me, even if they are a cell away, even if they are faint with hunger or cold with terror or choking almost to death they can hear ME, and I can hear THEM and we are one, we are *all one*

Banging on the door. The care home buzzers all start going off. Chaos building.

WARDER Stand away from the door prisoner D28686! STAND AWAY!

CONSTANCE And now – now they are coming for me.

She steels herself. The noise is unbearable.

Amid the chaos of Holloway and the panic of CONSTANCE and the banging of the doors, a booming of male voices 'Order, order!!' and booing while LORD VIC is making a speech in Parliament:

VICTOR As Lady Constance Lytton, my sister, who has a weak heart, was considered too ill to be force fed. Dressed as Jane Warton, a common woman, she is not. She has been through hell. She is magnificent, but make no mistake... This now is *war*.

CONSTANCE Now they are coming for me.

JADE   I won't go. I won't let them do it! They can't do it, it's against the law /now-

CONSTANCE You must go/ NOW!

As she pushes JADE through the window/door/ something similar JADE resists.

JADE   Come with me! Come now!

CONSTANCE Oh, no. I have never felt so free as in this place. So full of love for the others. I will not leave them. I am alive for the first time!

She starts the tapping again then grips JADE urgently.

CONSTANCE   Wait! Tell me – Do you believe it will ever happen, that women will one day get the vote?

JADE   Oh, but they – they already – Yes. It will happen.

CONSTANCE One day.

JADE   One day.

CONSTANCE No surrender! Now go!

The noise and terror builds. The buzzer too, constantly.

JADE   When we're coming in for a hard landing, there's often a bounceback and passengers don't know that it's usually fine because it feels like a volcano but you just have to – You have to *not panic*. You have to assume brace position. (*She demonstrates to CONSTANCE so they share this last terrible moment of anticipation.*) Hold yourself firm...

CONSTANCE Keep tight hold of yourself.

JADE   Be prepared for anything...

CONSTANCE Look after everyone around you and remember...

JADE As – We – Achieve – Hard – Impact –

CONSTANCE Remember the secret to surviving –

JADE What?

CONSTANCE The secret to surviving is –

JADE – is what?

CONSTANCE No surrender... no surrender... NO SURRENDER!

CONSTANCE braces herself as they rush in and JADE escapes.

No Surrender and incredible noise builds as JADE goes out the other side.

JADE leaves, looks around, disoriented. The buzzer sounds again impatiently as she tries to quickly work out which room.

JADE Sometimes, when we landed, I'd forget where I was. Minneapolis... Monaco... Morocco...

The airports blended into one after a while. My favourite was the one, I've forgotten which, their sign said, *Start here. Go anywhere...* But, Landing Lips, that was our saying. Lips and tips. (*She automatically checks her lipstick and nails and hair.*) Heels up. (*Checks her shoes. Desperately checking the rooms.*) We always had to put the stilettos on to clack through the airport. "*Never forget, you are always representing the airline.*" I like to keep my standards just as high in here. Higher.

A buzzer goes and JADE finds the room. She stops dead. It's GRANDA's old room. She touches the door number.

JADE   Not this one... Not this room...

She looks around to see if anyone else will come.

JADE   Hello? Any staff? Ruby? Jax?

But silence, apart from the buzzer. GRANDA appears, unseen and unheard by JADE.

JADE   I can't do it. I can't go in.

GRANDA   You can do it. You can do anything...

JADE   It's the last place you were on earth...

GRANDA   You must go where you are called, my pet lamb. It's the best job you ever had, isn't it?... And anyway... I'm not there anymore. I left nothing of myself there, my best girl.

JADE   I can't... I can't! All I can see is you, lying there like a stone.

GRANDA   You never know what you will find in life. But if you never try... Remember what we always said? When one of us goes... the other goes ON.

JADE closes her eyes and knocks.

JADE   Hello?

A young woman appears; BOUSHRA.

JADE   What can I help you with...

JADE reads the name on the door quickly, discreetly.

JADE   Mrs El-Aimeni?

BOUSHRA *(flatly)* No. That's my mother.

She looks around, gestures helplessly to the empty room, things in boxes.

BOUSHRA Was. *Was* my mother.

She turns away, not able to control herself.

BOUSHRA I wanted to let someone know I was - finished... With...

She gestures around the room; packing up a small box.

JADE has been discreetly wandering the room, looking at, touching surfaces, drawers, walls, as if trying to memorise everything... or look for something that might have been left behind... then she hears what BOUSHRA is saying.

JADE Was-

BOUSHRA She – she's gone. She –

JADE I'm so sorry!

She goes to touch BOUSHRA but BOUSHRA evades her, picking up a photograph of a woman in a flight cap.

BOUSHRA Never let your guard down, never let them see your weakness. She taught me well, my Mumma.

JADE Never look down...

BOUSHRA But sometimes, just sometimes, I wished she could be just a little bit proud of me.

She tells this as if it's happening now:

BOUSHRA There's only one woman in the pilot intake of four hundred and fifty ... four hundred and forty-nine men and me. I can't do it. I'll never do it. It's too big. I'll put people's lives at risk. I'll panic. I'm hyperventilating, Mumma! But she sits me down and brushes my hair, this always comforts me–

BOUSHRA becomes MUMMA.

MUMMA/BOUSHRA Boushra el-Aimeni. Are you going to give up on the one thing you have wanted since you were a tiny girl? Eh? Are you going to give up your heart's dream? Because why? What has changed? This morning you were singing like a bird in front of the mirror and now look at you? I don't say anything. What can I say? But she's clever, my Mumma. She *knows*.

BOUSHRA She stops dead, says: Did someone – say something? No one said anything, Mumma. I'm waiting, and she can *wait,* this woman.

It's nothing. It's *nothing*. But she always knows.

She tells me, 'Boushra. My Boushra. You can do anything if you want to. You can do *anything*. I couldn't, but you can. Remember that, the next time this *nothing* speaks to you. Hold up your head and look *nothing* in the eye and remember my voice'.

When we were doing our training we'd only ever been in the simulator. The cockpit size doesn't change when it comes to the real thing, but when I walked into the aircraft for the first time, I was like, 'Wow, this is *big*." It was like flying a building!

The men saw my face, and one of them said just loud enough for me to hear, *'Looks like she's gonna be sick. Maybe she should go to the Ladies. Oh, wait – there isn't a Ladies, is there? Because only men should be here!'*

It's true. There was no Ladies. I used to drink nothing all day and sometimes I'd feel as if I were going to pass out, when the temperature hit the high 40s. But I never did. I'd dig my nails into the palm of my hand until I could see straight again.

I look him in the eye.

I am no lady, I say. I am a *woman*. Please treat me with the respect and dignity you would treat your wives or your sisters. He looks at me thoughtfully, and I knew I'd got him. Then –

Oh, my wife wouldn't disgrace herself like you do, he says. *And my sister's not a whore.*

I didn't tell Mumma exactly what he said because... well. Mothers, you know? They will get even with anyone who messes with their daughters. But...

She thought that would be the end of it. She thought I would give up my dream. Settle down. Make her happy. But she always surprised me..

She switches into captain mode.

BOUSHRA Your flight today will be approximately three hours and thirty-eight minutes, due to land at 8pm local time. We have tail winds on our side so we may even make up some time. I'm Captain Boushra El-Aimeni, your pilot today and I hope you have a pleasant and comfortable flight.

There's usually a... little... flicker, like a shiver of unrest and excitement after this. I can feel it, sometimes even hear it in the cabin, but today, I hear a louder voice than usual. I ask my first officer what's happening.

'The usual rubbish. Some man said since women can't even drive cars... blah blah... why on earth are they being allowed to fly a plane, etcetera and he wants to get off, only – a woman shouted him down –'

'Wait a minute...' He listens. Smiles. Clears his throat.

'Uh... Captain', she's saying, 'That's my daughter in there, and she's got every right to fly this plane, and you sit down and have some respect. And he says, 'Oh-oh. I think we've got Mummy on board.'

Unbelievable. I try to forget and get on with my job. Just as I'm steadying the plane after takeoff, I hear her say: 'A round of applause, please, for our Captain, *my daughter,* who has taken off the plane safely.'

I'm completely – mortified. As if there was any doubt I'd lift the plane safely! But inside, inside, I'm grinning like a five-year-old for the entire rest of that flight. I never got a chance to tell her that... 'Our captain. My daughter.'

JADE   I think... I think she was very proud.

BOUSHRA picks up the photograph again and JADE looks at it.

JADE   You did it...

BOUSHRA   No. I *do* it. But you – you do this. I couldn't.

In their own ways, they both look round the room for the last time and leave, touching the door and saying goodbye silently.

BOUSHRA leaves – and salutes JADE as she does so. JADE makes one last tour of the room and picks up something.

JADE   You left something behind – oh, she's gone... (*She looks at it. It is pilot's wings... she puts them into her pocket as the buzzer goes and she goes to the 'magic' room saying*) 'Mrs Fisher!'

She's IMMEDIATELY rugby tackled to the ground by VIOLET who throws herself on top of her.

VIOLET   Don't speak.

JADE   What-

VIOLET   Keep very, very quiet and very, very still. Move back inside the tent as smoothly as you can and don't look behind you. Do as I say and don't ask why.

JADE crawls back inside the 'tent'.

JADE Why –?

VIOLET Tiger. Duck!

VIOLET shoots at the tiger.

VIOLET That'll teach him. Missed, but it's annoyed him. It usually is a he, on the prowl, looking for a mate. Now move slowly and carefully, and keep calm. Trust me, I know what I'm doing. I've travelled in every country of the world, chiefly for the purpose of scientific research... carried out archaeological studies among ruins of ancient civilisation, including Mesopotamia, Egypt, Afghanistan, Bolivia... Cairo to Cape, Lapland to Russia with reindeer and through Persia to Baluchistan... up the Amazon in a canoe, walked over the Andes 16,000ft into Peru, took the first motor transport from Addis Ababa to Nairobi, visited the Ethiopian and Eritrean war fronts... Mandalay to Peking overland, Turkey to Tibet by yak, and mule caravan... first English guest of the Chinese Communist party, spent five hours in a cave interviewing Mao, drove ambulances in the Middle East, the only woman. Travelled over the Turkish frontier into Iran, lived with the Russian Army... was flown from Iran to Washington, given the post of special correspondent to the *London Daily Express* and obviously displeased someone as I was sent back to China.

You?

JADE Me? I – you want me to – follow that?

VIOLET Well?

JADE I'm a – I *was* a flight attendant. Cabin crew. Assistant head of –

VIOLET   Oh, a gofer. Go for this, go for that.

JADE   I loved my job. Loved it. I was *never* a gofer. I was – I was all things and everything.

Now, I look after people on the ground. I'm grounded. I mean – I'm much more grounded.. it suits me... I – how can I help you?

VIOLET thrusts the gun at JADE.

VIOLET   Cover me

JADE   What for?

VIOLET   Hold the gun. I have to pee. Where's there's one tiger, there's more.

JADE   I won't shoot a tiger. I won't shoot anything!

VIOLET   Back me up. If I die, how do you get out of here? More importantly, I need to pee!

VIOLET pees very loudly.

JADE   Wow, you – you pee like a horse.

VIOLET   It helps to frighten the wildlife. Are you covering me? Just to let you know, where there's tigers there are often wolves. At this time of year, very common.

VIOLET howls. Waits.

VIOLET   No, nothing back. That's a good sign. The pack leader usually answers... You try. Like this –

She howls. JADE tries.

VIOLET   Rubbish

JADE tries again. It gets a response:

CHILD   Mama!

A child's demanding cry. VIOLET reacts, trying to juggle playing with toddlers while also searching for wolves.

CHILD Mama!

VIOLET Yes darling.

CHILD Mama! Play bricks with me.

VIOLET I can't, my darling, I'm in a cave.

CHILD Mama! Mama! Mama! Hide and seek!

VIOLET Hiding from *you*...

MR VIOLET Violet, where are my cufflinks?

VIOLET In China... Mexico... Chile... in the sink, darling.

MR VIOLET Haven't you had them polished?

VIOLET Russia... Singapore...

MR VIOLET Haven't you given the cook orders for the dinner party?

VIOLET I meant to but... the Amazon!

MR VIOLET The servants are waiting for their orders.

VIOLET The Andes... the Arctic... they were all there, waiting to be explored and I was in... Watford.

CHILD Mama!

MR VIOLET Violet!

SERVANT Madam?

MR VIOLET Where is my bloody wife this time?

VIOLET shakes JADE's hand.

VIOLET Who the hell are you anyway? I'm Violet Olivia Henley Fisher Cressy Marcks, you can call me any of those names, some belong to husbands, the rest all my own. You must be my new gofer. I'm afraid the last one died, I do wear them out so quickly, God rest his soul. I hope you're not afraid of snakes. Or caves. Or snakes in caves, often happens. A snake crawling over one at night is not a pleasant proposition. Once a wretched thing bit me below the knee... Having lanced the wound, I used a mirror to see if I was going black or grey... I decided on coffee, a walk and sleep, and if I was going to die... I was at peace with the world, so ... there was nothing to worry about. All I was really frightened of was my husband's letters:

MR VIOLET Now look here, Mrs Violet Olivia Henley Fisher Cressy Marcks, is it really too much trouble to ask you to return home for my new shop-opening ceremony? All the other wives will be there and people will talk, and by people, *yes dammit,* I mean the Mayor. You have now been away for seven months and a number of weeks, and the house has become rundown and disreputable. The children are difficult, frankly they appear to take after you and... Really, Violet, it is just insupportable! I have put up with as much as I can, but no man should be expected to –

VIOLET rustles the pages... reams... of the letter...

VIOLET ... much more in this vein, he does run on at the mouth rather.... always has, no wonder I stay away in Alaska... the Amazon...

MR VIOLET Alaska.... Polar bears... utter madness... terrible mother... Amazon... ropes! ...the children are running wild... on horseback up a creek!

VIOLET Are you done, dear?

MR VIOLET ... in a cave with Chairman Mao... Never live it down... and the damage to my career, but never mind that... Oh no, Mrs Violet must have her travelling, not satisfied with a week in a nice hotel in Eastbourne but she must ascend the bloody Andes SEVEN times!

VIOLET Are you done NOW, dear?

MR VIOLET Damn it all, Vi, I miss you in my bed!

Silence. VIOLET howls with surprise and maybe sadness...

VIOLET Oh! I don't know what to say, really. Husband, you do pick your times, don't you? One is currently up a mountain. Surrounded by wolves. Hungry wolves. Wolves that care nothing but for the hunt, the ceaseless hunt for something new, something *next,* wolves that are getting closer and closer, and I truly believe that by the time I have finished writing back to you, they will be at the door – at the flap of this tent, this flimsy piece of cloth...

Finally an answering howl. They huddle a tiny bit closer.

VIOLET Tigers... elephants... lions... snakes, I will take on but wolves, wolves hunt in a pack.

JADE A tiger can take down a wolf, surely?

VIOLET Ah, but a pack of wolves can take down a fully-grown tiger. Family, you see... they'll do anything to protect their own. But – it's been worth it. Every lonely, rain-soaked, dangerous, dusty, fetid, arid, febrile moment...

JADE All the violent storms, the pilots laughing, drunk, the handsy passengers, the alphas of the galley who won't let you join the pack, the sleepless nights worrying I'd be late for an early, or early for a late because I had no other life in my life, the moment when the engines died one by one, the angry skies humming with electricity, the bad feeling once the lightning strikes, it was all worth it...

For the view...

For the blue...

For the missing of you...

For the skies...

The night sky when no one but me and the crew were awake as we flew silently through the black and the blue and the silver of the stars and I'd watch the captains and I'd wonder... Oh I'd wonder, ALL RIGHT YES, I would wonder what it would be like to just –
Take control
For once
Steer
Be the one who –
The *one*.

VIOLET looks at JADE curiously.

VIOLET I was wrong about you... You're not scared, are you?

JADE I'm terrified.

A howl, closer.

VIOLET This is the only thing in the whole world that scares me... To look into those eyes and know I have met my match.

Wolves will do anything to protect their cubs.
Wonderful mothers.
And I... All I can do is – keep trying to outwit it, this *feeling*... This *duty of... love*.
Keep ahead...
Outrun my own pack.

Each time I leave them it gets harder.
Take my advice. Keep running and never –
Never
Look –
Back!

A child cries.

CHILD Mama!

Another howl. JADE looks out of the tent.

Another howl, very close.

JADE moves a few inches out...

VIOLET What are you doing? Stay inside!

JADE I've got to go.

VIOLET Awful creatures, they enjoy killing.

JADE Go out there...

VIOLET Tear your throat out, they take their time too. Don't look at them – don't look –

Then: JADE can't hear GRANDA...

GRANDA You can do it, lovey. You can do *anything*. Didn't I always tell you that? Trust your old Granda... You can do anything... Who are you going to be, I wonder... I wish I could be around to see...

JADE crawls further out.

VIOLET What are you doing? Are you mad?

JADE is mesmerised.

JADE Oh, it – it's – beautiful... It's the most beautiful thing I've ever – She, it must be a she, I don't know how I know this, but I do, I DO and she's looking right at me, and maybe this is how you go mad, maybe this is how it happens when you can't get over something. I don't know I DON'T KNOW but I think she sees me, she sees right into me...

JADE inches forward.

VIOLET Don't move... I'll give you the gun.

JADE She won't hurt me.

VIOLET Oh yes, she bloody well will! She'll smell you from a mile off as a predator with all that gunk on your face. And females are the worse, particularly if she's a mother –

JADE Give me a cloth.

VIOLET What?

JADE Quickly!

VIOLET jumps to it. JADE wipes her face roughly, almost violently, with a rough old towel and a basin of water, scrubbing the make-up off quickly.

VIOLET Don't look her in the /eyes oh too late...

JADE /much too late

VIOLET She's got you now in her sights, locked on.

JADE Her head tilted to one side, like she's trying to read me... Or ask me something... Tell me something...

VIOLET Eat you!

JADE Her mouth is open the tiniest bit, as if she's... It can't be – as if she's – smiling.

VIOLET Did you never read *Little Red Riding Hood*, you fool? Don't you remember –

JADE   I always thought the wolf was the best character…

VIOLET   You can't win--

JADE   Faster than a snake, wilder than a storm, older than time, eyes like a lake, fur like quicksilver…

I can feel her, my blood jumping inside my own body. My heart, it's beating again, it's beating… And – and all I want to do is cry… I want to cry and scream and laugh and –

Suddenly she howls. It's a proper, bloodcurdling howl, full of anger and love and calling and misery and joy.

JADE   I think I might still be alive, after all…

She moves nearer… and the wolf moves nearer to her… the howl is low now, a growl, almost a purr. Obviously the wolf is a metaphor… She reaches a hand out and gets closer.

A buzzer sounds but JADE ignores it.

She gets out the stone and shows it to the wolf.

JADE   I won't hurt you. Come closer… Or I… I will come to you… I've never been so scared in my life but… This is worth it.

VIOLET sighs, almost crying.

VIOLET   I think I'm going to need another gofer…

The buzzer goes, repeatedly. JADE wakes up, suddenly, stands up, jolted out of her dream.

JADE   I've got to go. How do I get back?

VIOLET   Back to where? This is the most beautiful place on earth. Why would anyone want to leave it?

JADE   I've got to go NOW.

VIOLET Go then. The only thing you need to know is –

JADE   I know what I need to do! I've got to GO!

VIOLET ducks left suddenly.

VIOLET Tiger to the left, no time to explain... Take THAT you arrogant bastard!

Shots are fired and VIOLET is gone.

JADE rushes into a room and finds JUNE, waiting, aviator's glasses on. They look at each other.

JADE is panting as if she's run a mile. She touches her own face, aghast.

JUNE   You're late.

JADE   I– I'm sorry. So sorry, June. I got lost...

JUNE   Chin up. Fly straight.

JADE takes JUNE outside. The stars are just coming out. The little plane is there. They watch it. JADE can't settle though.

JADE   June, something happened. Today, something –

JUNE   Every woman should learn to fly.

She looks directly at JADE for the first time.

JADE   Oh!... If only it was that easy.

JUNE   Do you miss it? Answer me.

JADE gets the stone out of her pocket, looks at it and hands it to JUNE.

JADE It's just a stone. *A stone is like a heart.* Granda had all these sayings that didn't always make sense to anyone but me... but this, this one, this last one... I don't understand – I don't understand it!

JADE is near to deep grief now. JUNE looks at her again, and then at the stone. She turns it over, carefully, and then nods.

JADE And it shouldn't matter, but it does! It does matter! Because I'm on my own now, forever. And I've jumped out of a hot air balloon to save it and been locked in a prison cell to keep it safe and nearly shot a tiger and faced a wolf – my – my wolf. And I still don't understand what it means!

JADE is nearly crying in her distress. JUNE touches her hand gently.

JUNE Look.

She holds the stone up to JADE.

JUNE A stone is like a heart...

JUNE puts the stone against her heart to show JADE.

JADE takes the stone. Something starts to turn over in her mind...

Through this next exchange, JUNE takes off the aviator's glasses and dies, quietly, in her chair, stargazing.

GRANDA and little JADE reprise from THEN:

JADE Look, Granda –

She gives him the stone.

JADE It's for you

GRANDA But what is it, my little love?

JADE   It's special. See?

They both examine it carefully.

GRANDA   I do see... I'll keep it safe my chickie-dee.

He fits it against his heart.

GRANDA   Take it, honey-pie. Keep it always with you. Keep it close to you... It meant the world to me. Take it wherever you go. Until you don't need it anymore...

JADE fits it against her own heart.

She looks at JUNE and after a long, painful moment, realises what has happened.

JADE   Oh June... June. I didn't get to tell you –yes, I miss it. (*She sits holding JUNE's hands.*) But you knew that.

She might give in to despair. She's lost someone else important. But:

The WOMEN appear around JADE to give her courage. They chivvy and bolster and nudge her into action...

CONSTANCE   No surrender. You're nearly there.

VIOLET   Now: pack!

They help her dress in her new uniform.

DOLLY   Now, check the ropes!

CONSTANCE   Now stand firm and sing –

VIOLET   Remember, you actually need very little –

CONSTANCE   Just one good friend, whoever they may be –

VIOLET   Yourself.

DOLLY The right song.

CONSTANCE The right words.

VIOLET Don't look back.

DOLLY Don't listen to them when they say, don't look down, because the view is the best bit, wherever you look.

VIOLET The only thing you really need to know is–

CONSTANCE Don't wait any longer…

A new day.

JADE looks in a mirror. She is now dressed in a pilot's uniform.

Looks at us in a very honest, direct way.

JADE I love my job.
My new job.
It's probably the best job I've ever had.
Although the last one turned out to be pretty good…
But – this – I don't know how this'll turn out!

Puts her flight hat on. Deep breath.

JADE Eyes straight ahead.

All the women are there beside her now.

Then:

JADE Who do you think the pilot is, Granda?

Granda chuckles. Small JADE follows the plane with her eyes.

Now: JADE is now by a sparkling sea. A small plane can be heard, overhead.

She looks up, follows it with her gaze.

JADE I miss you. I'll always miss you.
Wherever I am, no matter how old I get, no matter what happens to me from now on until the end of time.
Because...
You were my everything...
Always and in all ways.
But you'll never leave me.
(She turns the stone heart over in her hands.)
I know that now.
And this... this is *now*. This is new.

She places the stone down on the sea shore.

She puts JUNE's aviator's glasses on.

But before, she winks at us.

Lights down.

The End.

ABOUT THE PRODUCTION

Genesis of the Project
Thomas Kell

Chair of Trustees

If you are reading this whilst sitting in the departure lounge of an airport, perhaps forlornly glancing up at departure boards strewn with red notices of delay; or, actually on a plane but which seems to be endlessly circling amidst talk of 'issues' at air traffic control, then, we at Pursued by a Bear share your pain! It took many years to get *Nothing on Earth* airborne, largely due to the unwelcome arrival of the Covid-19 pandemic. Our theatre sector underwent major upheaval; patterns and habits of making and experiencing theatre were shattered. Lives were upended, funding was in even shorter supply, different stories were wanted.

We had begun to develop *Nothing on Earth* in 2018, following commissioning of the script from Anna Reynolds. An initial draft of the play was presented at Pursued by a Bear's Foundry festival that year. Extensive R&D, funded by Arts Council England, took place in 2019. This included public readings hosted by partners Hertford Theatre and Trestle. These also allowed testing of participatory activity such as singing and reminiscence theatre which became integral to the project.

Plans for a tour in 2020 were curtailed by Covid. Whilst the world was in hibernation, commissions from UH Arts + Culture and Dacorum Borough Council and a grant from ACE's Covid Emergency Response Fund enabled the filming of six *Nothing on Earth* shorts newly written by

ABOUT THE PRODUCTION 87

Reynolds and again inspired by the themes of *Nothing on Earth*. These films, which, true to PBAB's mission, featured contributions from artists based throughout the UK and in Trinidad and Sri Lanka, are available online via the company's website.

A new tour was arranged for Women's History Month 2023. Pre-existing partnerships were revived and significant new relationships formed. Funding was awarded by Arts Council England and, seven years after Hertfordshire's Hidden Heroines, a cast and creative team assembled for rehearsals at Chats Palace.

Whilst performances came to an end on 1 April 2023, the project continues through new films and this publication.

I wonder what aircraft engineers feel when a new design hurtles into the sky. Nerves, surely; pride, hopefully. As we launched *Nothing on Earth* into the deeply uncertain 2023 environment of live performance our hearts were in our mouths. To see it soar has been immensely fulfilling. Reactions have been amongst the most positive we have ever encountered. It has been a delight to bring this remarkable play to audiences. In turn their engagement has refuelled us and renewed our love for this artform. We are grateful to all who share our journeys.

Creating the Production
Rosamunde Hutt

From 2019 to 2023 we gathered with elders in Hertfordshire and Hackney, and heard their memories of lives lived in their local communities and beyond, and of the incredible women they had known, mothers, grandmothers, sisters and aunts. We listened to tales of migration, travel, hardship, caring, and above all of hope and resilience.

On tour with *Nothing on Earth* in Women's History Month 2023 we shared these compelling stories with our audiences. In Dorchester and Hackney local singers delighted audiences as they joined in with our cast in performance, and sang two thrilling Suffragette anthems.

Anna's playful, poignant and uplifting play was the springboard for this community involvement. Uncovering these stories and celebrating these women's voices is part and parcel of the *Nothing on Earth* experience.

The focus of the piece was forever shifted with the pandemic. Anna had always talked of bringing to light unheard voices and hidden histories. That goal deepened when we realised that many voices of the nation's elders were being lost, and stories that might have been told could not now be heard. The play altered in leaps and bounds. New characters came out of the wings; June, quietly sitting in the corner of a care home, suddenly reveals that she used to fly Spitfires; May, with a triumphant story to tell about her giant leap from serving in the Co-op to building a bomber; Boushra, an airline pilot, encouraged to take flight by her indomitable mother who told her 'I couldn't but you can'.

And as we sat out Covid-19 the production was developing apace.

Designer Sophia Lovell Smith was creating a light-footed nimble ingenious set, in her words – 'characters colliding in space and time', a world on wheels with steel mesh and colourful cloth, bringing to life the care home, the hot air balloon, the cell, the tent, and planes old and new. She generated a sense of perpetual movement, with costumes and props being handed from performer to performer, umbrellas signifying flight, and hard-edged shelving units creating cockpits one minute and linen cupboards the next.

Composer Helen Chadwick, set key moments and motifs to music, creating beautiful solos, such as 'I'm flying, across the earth', sung by June, our Spitfire pilot, and 'Sky Tall', sung by May in her Welsh factory; *a capella* songs sung by the cast, wrapping Dolly and Jade in music as they parachute down through the clouds, 'Floating and Falling'; and encapsulating the central themes of the piece for example with 'This Love'. In the closing moments of the show our central character Jade comes to terms with loss and change as the three Heroines sing 'Wherever you are in the World, I will be with you'.

Joined by lighting designer Holly Ellis, who created vivid contrasts between magical worlds and the real world, and subtle shifts between past and present, through an evocative use of colour and light; and sound designer Anna Short, delivering both the everyday sounds of planes, of the hot air balloon being fired up, of buzzers ringing for help and attention in the care home, and richly textured soundscapes, for example, of prison life, with doors clanging shut, and the threat and the fear of force feeding and cruelty ever present. And Emily Gray, movement director, finding a visceral physical language of being grounded and then in flight, and of the mystery and wonder of the wolves that Jade confronts and engages with in the wilderness.

And so *Nothing on Earth* came to life celebrating intrepid women of courage. But thanks to our reminiscence work, we celebrate also the quiet heroines, and heroes too, the Chinese woman who learnt English by watching *Countdown,* the mother who picked herself up after her house was reduced to rubble in the London Blitz, the father who joined the Jarrow Marches for a new life. And of course in *Nothing on Earth* the ranks of carers who look after our elders day and night. These sit alongside Dolly, Constance and Violet as lives well lived. If I go to a museum I now look for a photo of a suffragette or if I pass an old lady on the street I wonder what her journey has been. The play pays tribute to them all.

Composing the Music
Helen Chadwick

Anna's script has so many images and ideas to turn into song or very short snippets of song that can come seamlessly out of the spoken text and back into it without slowing the play down. These sung bursts of energy, heard before or after they are spoken, give a drive and playfulness to the scenes. Attached to melody, rhythm and the emotionality of song, key ideas are thus embedded deeper into the bodies and memories of the public.

The cornerstone song is 'Once They Are Aroused' from a speech by Emmeline Pankhurst which Constance Lytton quotes in the play. Here is my version...

Once They Are Aroused

Emmeline Pankhurst
Helen Chadwick

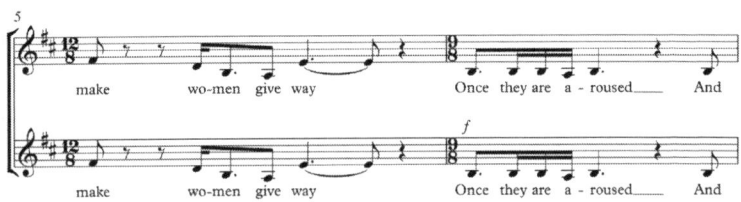

ABOUT THE PRODUCTION

NOTHING ON EARTH
by Anna Reynolds

First performance at South Mill Arts Centre on International Women's Day, 8 March 2023

Cast

Sarah Agha	Dolly, Boushra
Lebogang Fisher	Jade
Joanna Foster	Constance, June
Lincoln James	Granda, Monsieur, Lord Victor, Mr Violet
Rhiannon Meades	Violet, May, Aunty

All other parts played by the company.

Creative Team

Director	Rosamunde Hutt
Composer	Helen Chadwick
Designer	Sophia Lovell Smith
Lighting Designer	Holly Ellis
Sound Designer	Anna Short
Movement Director	Emily Gray
Production Manager	Crin Claxton
Company Stage Manager	Jack Scanlon

Production Team

Rachel Barker	Associate Producer and Project Manager
Mitch Broomhead	Relighter
Joanna Foster	Singing Captain / Workshop Leader
Charlotte Furness	Marketing Consultant (Leviart Marketing Ltd)
Donna Heath	Graphic Design
Karene Horner-Hughes	Workshop Leader
Thomas Kell	Supervisory Producer
Nancy Poole	PR
Steph Pyne Design	Graphic Design Main Concept
Géhane Strehler	Associate Artist / Workshop Leader
Grant Watson	Film Associate
Greta Zabulyte	Production Photography

Biographies are available at www.pursuedbyabear.co.uk

ABOUT THE PRODUCTION

The Tour

8 March
South Mill Arts Centre, Bishop's Stortford, Hertfordshire

12 March
Trestle Arts Base, St Albans, Hertfordshire

15 March
Welwyn Garden City Library, Welwyn Garden City, Hertfordshire

16 March
Watford Central Library, Watford, Hertfordshire

17 March
Hertfordshire County Hall, Hertford, Hertfordshire

18 March
Yvonne Arnaud Theatre, Guildford

22 March
Watersmeet, Rickmansworth, Hertfordshire

24 March
Dorchester Corn Exchange, Dorchester

25 March
Artsreach at Corfe Castle, Wareham, Dorset

29 March
Old Town Hall, Hemel Hempstead, Hertfordshire

30 March – 1 April
Chats Palace, Hackney, London

WORKSHOP RESOURCES

NOTHING ON EARTH REMINISCENCE WORKSHOP PLAN

by Karene Horner-Hughes, Rosamunde Hutt & Géhane Strehler

The workshop is based around the play using its themes and characters to unlock testimony from workshop participants. It can be adjusted to suit a group as required, in educational and community settings. The workshop is especially appropriate for elders.

Welcome

Introduce the themes of the play and of the workshop:

- Heroines from the past and the present.
- Home.
- Tales of travel and migration.
- Historical Heroines.

Ask participants to talk to the person next to them and ask who is their Historical Heroine, and why. Offer some examples, e.g. 'Joan of Arc', 'Rosa Parks'.

Ask pairs to introduce their partner to the group and announce their partner's heroine and the reason for choosing her.

Fairy Godmother

- Remind the group of the story of the Fairies bestowing gifts upon Sleeping Beauty, e.g. grace, generosity, wit, song, and dance.
- Present a baby doll, wrapped in a shawl, and pass her around the room. Ask if you could gift this 'child' with personality traits to be a successful, dynamic, empowered woman, what would you grant her?

Would You Rather

- Pose participants three questions, encourage quick instinctive answers, and a brief chat on why they make their choices.
- Would you rather stay at home and stay safe OR speak out and risk prison?
- Would you rather stay at home and build a family OR explore the world and the dangers that come with that?
- Would you rather keep a steady job OR run away to join the circus?

Hertfordshire Heroines

Describe the heroines who appear in the play.

DOLLY SHEPHERD

The amazing Dolly Shepherd, born in Potters Bar in 1886, who became a daredevil aerial artist, thrilling crowds all over the land as she parachuted down from rickety hot air balloons.

CONSTANCE LYTTON

The incredibly brave Lady Constance Lytton, who lived at Knebworth House, fought passionately for Votes for Women and alongside other Suffragettes was force fed in Holloway Prison.

VIOLET CRESSY-MARCKS

The fearless Violet Cressy-Marcks who left her home in Bushey, and travelled around the world, trekking across Africa, canoeing up the Amazon and driving ambulances in World War Two.

REMINISCENCE
Home, Travel and Heroines

Work in small groups and encourage the sharing of reminiscences:
- When did you move to your community e.g. your village, town, county? Where did you come from? Why did you come?
- What do you like about living here?
- Write or talk about places lived and travelled. What is home?
- Which women have you admired? In your life, family, community?
- What do you remember about them? Why do they inspire you?
- Share oral histories, personal experiences and anecdotes.
- Workshop facilitators write the stories down.

Advice for the Future – Granda says

Briefly explain the journey of Jade and Granda. He has brought her up and is always giving Jade advice, encouraging her to 'go out there and live; and to 'take your chances, chucky egg...let the wind take you where it will... Trust your old granda, you can do *anything*' (pages 46-47).

What advice would you give today's young women?

THREE EXERCISES INSPIRED BY THE PLAY

Up Up and Away

- Read DOLLY's words about floating off in her balloon (page 40). When she flies she talks about her desire to disappear into the sky and leave material physical world behind - 'I am too high for the birds. Just me, free.'
- What would you gladly leave behind floating up, up and away in your balloon?

Look at All That Life Out There

- When CONSTANCE is in Holloway Prison she says 'Look at all that...life out there that everyone else is living!' (page 11).
- Write a stream of consciousness exercise completing Constance's statement

Just Stuff Everything in the Bloody Bag and Get Out of Here!

- Remind participants of VIOLET's extensive adventures and her longing for 'The Amazon! The Andes...the Arctic...they were all out there, waiting to be explored' (page 73).
- Write an 8 line poem celebrating extraordinary travels taken by yourself or your family.

SONGS

Teach 'The March Of The Women', a Suffragette anthem by Dame Ethel Smyth, music and lyrics available online.

Teach 'Once We Are Aroused', music by Helen Chadwick, words by Emmeline Pankhurst, available in this play text.

RECORD THE REMINSCENCES AND CREATIVE WRITING

After the workshop weave together all the reminiscences gathered and examples of creative writing. In a return visit share the collective contributions with the group. The reminiscences could be compiled into a book, accompanied by photos of the participants, or spoken in a digital film with accompanying images of the locality, historical heroines and the workshop participants.

PRODUCTION PHOTOS

Sarah Agha (Dolly) Photo: Greta Zabulyte

Lebogang Fisher (Jade) and Lincoln James (Granda) Photo: Greta Zabulyte

PRODUCTION PHOTOS

Joanna Foster (June) Photo: Greta Zabulyte

Rhiannon Meades (May) and Lebogang Fisher (Jade)
Photo: Greta Zabulyte

PRODUCTION PHOTOS

Sarah Agha (Boushra) Photo: Greta Zabulyte

Joanna Foster (June), Lebogang Fisher (Jade) Photo: Greta Zabulyte

Lebogang Fisher (Jade), Lincoln James (Monsieur), Sarah Agha (Dolly), Rhiannon Meades (Violet) Photo: Greta Zabulyte

Pursued By A Bear

We are a theatre and digital media company in residence at Trestle Arts Base in St Albans.

The company was founded by actor Joseph Millson, actor and director Stuart Mullins and the writer Craig Baxter in 1998 to produce exciting new writing with a global focus. We've worked nationally, internationally and locally with audiences in Cambridgeshire, London, Surrey and now Hertfordshire.

Our mission at PBAB is to champion women's playwriting and female theatre artists. In addition to this commission for Anna Reynolds we have begun the development of two new plays by Afia Nkrumah.

We accompany our theatre activity with programmes of participation and trans-media storytelling. Please check our website and social media for latest projects.

www.pursuedbyabear.co.uk

Artistic Director: Rosamunde Hutt
Associate Director (Film): Grant Watson
Associate Artists: Oladipo Agboluaje; Géhane Strehler
Trustees: Katherine Ives, Thomas Kell (Chair), Katy Silverton, Dr Adam Smith
Independent Examiner / Accountancy Advice (until May 2023): Charles Barker-Benfield, FCA (Morchard Bishop & Co.)

Pursued By A Bear Productions Ltd
Registered Charity No. 1091842
A Limited Company Registered in England & Wales, No. 3800928
Registered Address: Trestle Arts Base, Russet Drive, St Albans AL4 0JQ (UK)
info@pursuedbyabear.co.uk
Find us on social media @pbabproductions

COMPANY INFORMATION 111

Production Acknowledgements

The production and this publication would not have been possible without grant funding from Arts Council England. We are grateful.

We are also grateful for generous sponsorship for this publication from UH Arts + Culture, School of Creative Arts, University of Hertfordshire.

Nothing on Earth was created with the assistance of South Mill Arts Centre, Trestle, Dacorum Borough Council, Three Rivers District Council, Hertfordshire Libraries and Archives Service, Chats Palace.

Workshops featuring singing, reminiscences and writing took place in many locations both during and after the tour. A curtain-raiser 'Women of Courage', formed from memories contributed during workshops, was performed before *Nothing on Earth* in Hemel Hempstead and Hackney.

Thanks

Sue Scott Davison and all at South Mill Arts Centre; Helen Barnett, Clare Winter, Rhian Smith, Joe Martin at Trestle Arts Base; Rebekah Nicolas, Ros Cloke and the library managers and colleagues at Hertfordshire Libraries; Julie Gregson, Janice Brooker, Angela Ludlow, LLinos Thomas, Serena Williams, Millie Martin and colleagues at Hertfordshire Archives and Local Studies and County Hall; Alex Care, Annie Smith, Katie Ellis, Bryony Hedley and all at Dacorum Borough Council; Elaine Johnson, Bethany Barrett and all at Three Rivers District Council; Paula van Hagen, Perdie Bargh, Crin Claxton and all at Chats Palace; Tangle and Eve Oakley (generous loans); Géhane Strehler for immense support and input over so many years and for permission to use her image as the Aviatrix (in a photo by Ian Phillips).

Pursued by a Bear worked to produce *Nothing on Earth* since 2016. We have received enormous help from many brilliant organisations and individuals including: Suzanne Ahmet, Nia Davies, Ebony Feare, Chanel Glasgow, Safiyya Ingar, Hazel Maycock, Jane Nash, Shalini Peiris, Dale Superville (actors); Emily Gray, Annabel Lucas; Irma Inniss; Rhys Thomas & Hertford Theatre; Inna Allen, Melissa Alexander and colleagues at UH Arts + Culture, School of Creative Arts.

Aurora Metro Books

ADA by Emily Holyoake
ISBN 978-1-912430-09-3   £9.99

THREE WOMEN by Matilda Velevitch
ISBN 978-1-912430-35-2   £9.99

PROJECT XXX by Kim Wiltshire & Paul Hine
ISBN 978-1-906582-55-5   £8.99

COMBUSTION by Asif Khan
ISBN 978-1-911501-91-6   £9.99

DIARY OF A HOUNSLOW GIRL by Ambreen Razia
ISBN 978-0-9536757-9-1   £8.99

SPLIT/MIXED by Ery Nzaramba
ISBN 978-1-911501-97-8   £10.99

A GIRL WITH A BOOK by Nick Wood
ISBN 978-1-910798-61-4   £12.99

THE TROUBLE WITH ASIAN MEN by Sudha Bhuchar, Kristine Landon-Smith and Louise Wallinger
ISBN 978-1-906582-41-8   £8.99

WOMEN OF ASIA by Asa Palomera
ISBN 978-1-906582-94-4   £7.99

HARVEST by Manjula Padmanabhan
ISBN 978-0-9536757-7-7   £6.99

I HAVE BEFORE ME A REMARKABLE DOCUMENT by Sonja Linden
ISBN 978-0-9546912-3-3   £7.99

NEW SOUTH AFRICAN PLAYS ed. Charles J. Fourie
ISBN 978-0-9542330-1-3   £11.99

BLACK AND ASIAN PLAYS Anthology introduced by Afia Nkrumah
ISBN 978-0-9536757-4-6   £12.99

SOUTHEAST ASIAN PLAYS ed. Cheryl Robson and Aubrey Mellor
ISBN 978-1-906582-86-9   £16.99

SIX PLAYS BY BLACK AND ASIAN WOMEN WRITERS ed. Kadija George
ISBN 978-0-9515877-2-0   £12.99

www.aurorametro.com